New York City
CURIOSITIES

Help Us Keep This Guide Up to Date

Every effort has been made by the author and editors to make this guide as accurate and useful as possible. However, many things can change after a guide is published— establishments close, phone numbers change, facilities come under new management, and so on.

We would appreciate hearing from you concerning your experiences with this guide and how you feel it could be improved and kept up to date. While we may not be able to respond to all comments and suggestions, we'll take them to heart, and we'll also make certain to share them with the author. Please send your comments and suggestions to the following address:

GPP
Reader Response/Editorial Department
P.O. Box 480
Guilford, CT 06437

Or you may e-mail us at:
editorial@globepequot.com

Thanks for your input, and happy travels!

Curiosities Series

New York City
CURIOSITIES

Quirky characters,
roadside oddities &
other offbeat stuff

Lisa Montanarelli

Guilford, Connecticut

The prices, rates, and hours listed in this guidebook were confirmed at press time. We recommend, however, that you call establishments to obtain current information before traveling.

Photos by Lisa Montanarelli

Maps: Daniel Lloyd © Morris Book Publishing, LLC

Text design: Bret Kerr

Project editor: Ellen Urban

Layout artist: Casey Shain

Library of Congress Cataloging-in-Publication Data is available on file.

ISBN 978-0-7627-6055-8

Printed in the United States of America

10 9 8 7 6 5 4 3 2 1

contents

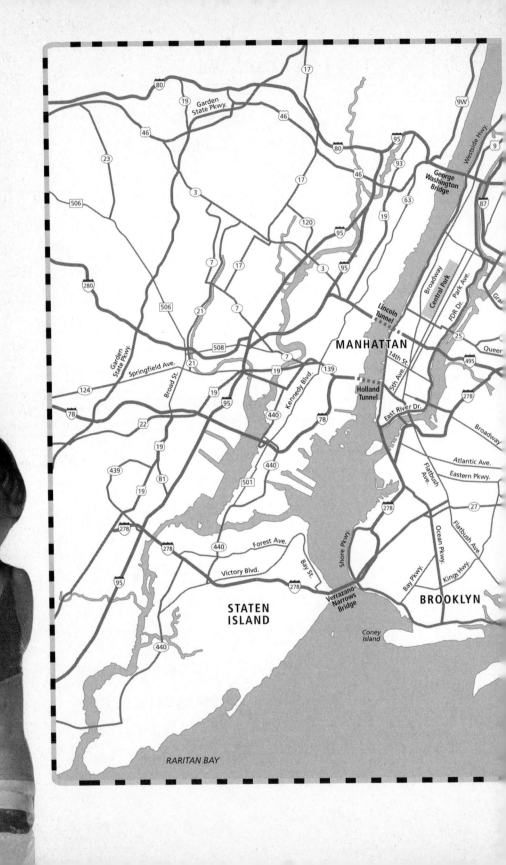

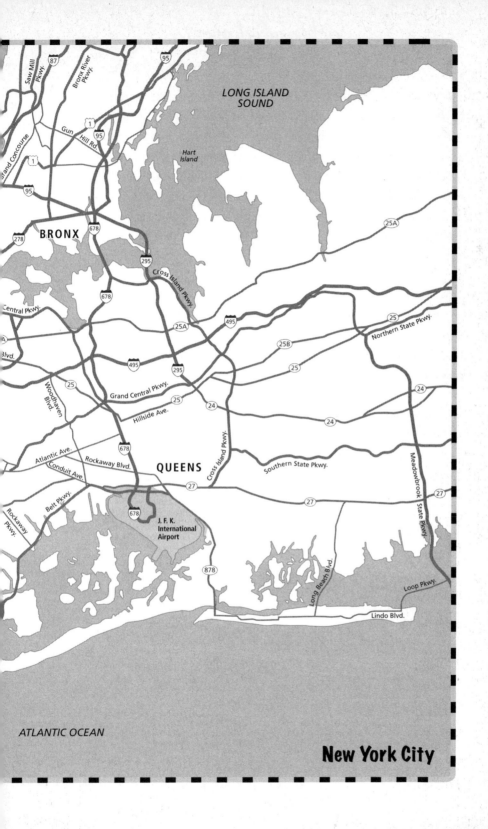

New York City

acknowledgments

I'd like to thank my editor, Meredith Rufino, for her enthusiasm, insights, and flexibility. Robert Lawrence offered traveling companionship, feedback on chapters, and unflagging support, while Bobby Morgan took great photos for the book. My thanks also go to Pamela Madsen, who introduced me to Chinatown in Flushing and M&I International Food in Brighton Beach; to Rob Hollander, who took me on a first-rate tour of Five Points; and to Shelly Mars, who listened to drafts and gave encouragement. Smokey Belles Catskills Residency, founded by Anie Stanley, provided an idyllic setting for this project in its final throes.

Artist Zoe Beloff, Danny Valdes of Reverend Billy and the Church of Life After Shopping, Bonnie McCourt of the Garibaldi-Meucci Museum, Barbara Mitchell of the Morris-Jumel Mansion, and David Picerno and Felicity Biel of Historic Richmond Town all helped with photos and photo permissions.

Finally, I'm grateful to the authors, bloggers, podcasters, and other NYC aficionados who have gone before me and provided invaluable resources for writing this alternative guide: Marci Reaven and Steve Zeitlin (*Hidden New York* and City Lore, www.citylore.org), Suzanne Reisman (*Off the Beaten [Subway] Track*), Greg Young and Tom Meyers (The Bowery Boys, www.theboweryboys.blogspot.com), Eric Ferrara (Lower East Side History Project, www.leshp.org), Rob Hollander (www .savethelowereastside.blogspot.com), Jeremiah Moss (Jeremiah's Vanishing New York, www.vanishingnewyork.blogspot.com), and Kevin Walsh (Forgotten New York, www.forgotten-ny.com), to name only a few.

introduction

★ ★

*T*his isn't your average guide to New York City. Forget about the Statue of Liberty. I'll show you to the monument with the most fondled testicles. We'll forgo *Zagat*'s top restaurants and chow down with robotic werewolves, mad scientists, and recently resurrected bartenders. And leave your Barneys charge card at home. We'll visit a supply store for superheroes with X-ray glasses, Wonder Woman–style Deflector Bracelets, and Evil Blob Containment Capsules.

You'll also get to know

- The ghost of a Broadway impresario who died in 1931 but still pinches actresses' butts
- A secret Chinatown tunnel converted into an underground strip mall, featuring the office of the consultant who feng shui'd the Trump International Tower
- A former landfill that was once the largest man-made structure on Earth, with trash piled higher than the Statue of Liberty
- Hip-hop celebrities who give bus tours of hip-hop landmarks
- And many other uncommon attractions.

A word about transportation: Getting around NYC can be difficult and costly, but a bit of Web sleuthing can reduce the headaches and expense. In the Big Apple, public transit is often the fastest route between any two points, and most sites in this book lie within reach of the subway and a brief walk or bus ride. For Staten Island locations, take the Staten Island Ferry and Railway.

For seasoned riders as well as neophytes, Hopstop (www.hopstop .com), MTA Trip Planner (www.tripplanner.mta.info/_start.aspx), and Google Maps (www.maps.google.com) allow you to enter your starting point and destination address and will provide door-to-door directions and an estimated travel time for subways, buses, regional rail, and walking. Subway construction and service changes are common on weekends, so be sure to check the MTA service advisories (www.tripplanner .mta.info/serviceAdvisory) before you leave your apartment or hotel. You can also pick up a free MTA subway map at any station with an information booth.

introduction

If you drive and don't have GPS, Google Maps (www.maps.google .com) gives detailed directions and allows you to view the surrounding streets, zoom in and out, and survey the area by satellite or street view. Parking in Manhattan is tricky, even if you're usually blessed with stellar parking karma. If you park on the street, be sure to inspect all signs and sacrifice quarters to the meter gods so you won't be ticketed or towed.

Caveat emptor: Not all parking garages are equal. Sometimes there's a $10 difference between garages a few blocks apart. If you're driving to a Manhattan destination, check www.bestparking.com for a map that shows nearby parking garages, allows you to compare rates, and offers advance reservations and coupons. Parking is less costly in the other boroughs and in some northern Manhattan neighborhoods, like Harlem, Washington Heights, and Inwood.

Finally, before you visit museums and other sites that might be closed to the public, call to make sure they still exist and that they're open at the hours you plan to go. The Web site might not be up-to-date, so your best bet is to pick up the phone. Since many museums and historic sites survive on donations from people like you, please give if you can.

Happy travels!

1

Downtown Manhattan
(South of Fourteenth Street)

In Downtown Manhattan, *it's easy to get lost in history—and in irregular street patterns. As the oldest part of NYC, the downtown predates the Commissioners' Plan of 1811, which dictated that all the streets from Houston to 155th Street (except those in Greenwich Village) would be laid out in an inflexible grid of east-west streets and north-south avenues. This made the city much easier to navigate, but it also entailed leveling hills, filling in streams, and converting the bountiful woodland landscape into a giant sheet of graph paper.*

Manhattan's southern tip, now called the Financial District, was once the Dutch settlement of New Amsterdam. After the British took over and renamed the city New York, they laid out Wall Street along the course of a wall that had once protected New Amsterdam's northern edge.

In the 1800s, NYC became a capital of industry and welcomed immigrants, largely because industrialists wanted an endless cheap labor supply. The immigrants settled on the site of a once freshwater lake, which had been glutted with sewage, tannery waste, and landfill. Unflappable speculators built tenement buildings on the sinking, reeking swamp, and charged exorbitant rents to immigrants just off the boat. The result was Five Points—possibly the most densely populated slum on Earth at the time.

In Five Points the immigrants lived in squalor—without heat, gaslight, or sewers—but the unprecedented mixing of people from so many

★ ★

different cultures and nations spawned some of the most famous neighborhoods in the world. Through much of the twentieth century, Downtown Manhattan continued to draw immigrants, as well as writers, artists, and iconoclasts. Manhattan's Chinatown is still the largest Chinese-American community in the United States. The Lower East Side once had the world's largest Jewish community. From the late nineteenth through the mid-twentieth century, Greenwich Village served as a bohemian Mecca and East Coast cradle of the Beat movement.

NYC still draws immigrants and artists, but most can no longer afford to live in Downtown Manhattan. Instead, they settle in Brooklyn and Queens, which have become the new downtown.

George Washington's Tooth
Fraunces Tavern

Manhattan's oldest building, Fraunces Tavern, survived three hundred years of frenetic urban development and still stands at 54 Pearl Street—exactly where Étienne Delancey built it in 1719.

Here's a sampling of the history that took place at Fraunces: The New York Chamber of Commerce was founded there in 1768. The Sons of Liberty plotted the New York Tea Party there in 1774. In 1775 a British cannonball flew through the roof. From 1776 to 1783 the British occupied NYC and forced poor Samuel Fraunces, the tavern's owner, to cook for them. After the British evacuated New York in 1783, Governor George Clinton threw a huge party at Fraunces for General George Washington, the commander-and-chief of the Continental Army. On December 4, 1783, Washington invited his officers to the tavern, bade them tearful farewell, and resigned his military post.

The building now houses Manhattan's only museum of the American Revolution. I'm personally not much of a war-history enthusiast. (I'm all for liberty and equality, but I find it hard to get excited about bloodshed, so there's always part of me that thinks, Hey, Canada freed itself from British tyranny without a bloody revolution. Why couldn't we?) Nonetheless, the museum satisfied my yen for history. In 2009 it was very exciting to see the 1215 Magna Carta, which rarely leaves England's Lincoln Cathedral, on display. The tavern also features period furnishings, Revolutionary War paintings, and a slew of George Washington portraits, memorabilia, and relics.

Yes, *relics*. One display case flaunts a sprig of Washington's hair (which was medium brown under those powdered white wigs) and what looked like a mother-of-pearl pendant for a necklace. The card read TOOTH FRAGMENT, donated by Washington's dentist, Dr. John Greenwood.

The father of our country had only one tooth left when he was inaugurated as president. He suffered from chronic toothaches—described at length in his diaries—and was on an endless quest for more comfortable dentures. Dr. Greenwood made him five sets from hippopotamus tusk, gold, elephant ivory—even human teeth. Fortunately, these were not the teeth of enemies killed in battle. As much as our forefathers loved the ancient Romans, they didn't adopt the Roman custom of stealing teeth from the heads of slain enemies and using them to make dentures.

Visit Fraunces Tavern between noon and 5:00 p.m. Monday through Saturday at 54 Pearl Street, or on the Web at www.fraunces tavernmuseum.org.

I wanted a shot of George Washington's tooth fragment,
but the museum strictly forbids photography.

Manhattan's Most Fondled Monument

Charging Bull

At the northern tip of Bowling Green Park, the eleven-foot-tall bronze bull flares his nostrils and twists back on his haunches. Each weekday morning, Wall Street traders stop to stroke the bronze basketballs hanging from his groin. This gesture supposedly brings good luck in the stock market. Millions of hands have burnished the genitalia to a shiny gold—brighter than the surrounding bronze. Hundreds upon thousands of tourists have posed with the lucky testicles, then sent their scrotum-rubbing photos home to family and friends around the globe.

Strangely enough, the city never commissioned *Charging Bull*. Arturo Di Modica, a well-heeled Sicilian-born artist, put $360,000 of his own cash into creating the sculpture—supposedly to celebrate the stock market's comeback after the 1987 crash. In the wee hours of December 15, 1989, Di Modica and friends installed the Colossus outside the New York Stock Exchange under a Christmas tree in the middle of Broad Street. The next morning, Wall Street awoke to the surprise gift. Since the seven-thousand-pound bull was blocking traffic, the cops treated it like an illegally parked car and hauled it to the city tow. A public outcry arose, until finally the city agreed to give the bull a permanent home at the northern tip of Bowling Green Park.

Years later, Di Modica offered to sell the piece to the city. The municipal government refused—not wanting to give other artists the

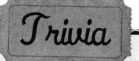

Trivia

In NYC 8.3 million people live in 304.8 square miles. We get along rather well, for people who live on top of each other.

5

★ ★

**Tourists are so smitten with the bull that it's
hard to photograph him in daylight.**

notion that they could leave their three-and-a-half-ton sculptures in
public places, then ask the city to foot the bill.

If you'd like to visit the bronze beastie, nighttime is best. I couldn't
get close during daylight hours, when crowds of tourists surround the
bull, snap pictures, and vie to cop a feel. So I returned to the deserted
financial district on a Sunday night and discovered—quite by accident—that late-night carousers find themselves irresistibly drawn to
the glistening orbs. No wonder the bull looks harassed.

Since I couldn't get near *Charging Bull* by day,
I returned at night.

Ticker-Tape Parades

During recent Ticker-Tape Parades up Broadway, frenzied stockbrokers
have been known to hurl open their office windows and fling their
clients' entire portfolios into the howling crowds below.

Why such madness? And what is a "Ticker-Tape Parade" anyway?
From roughly 1870 to 1970, stock prices were transmitted over telegraph lines. A machine called a stock ticker printed abbreviated company names and stock prices on long strips of paper called ticker tape.

The first Ticker-Tape Parade arose spontaneously on October 28,
1886—the day a rather famous copper lady was unveiled in the New
York Harbor. (The one with the torch, in case you haven't figured
that out.) Jubilant New Yorkers marched through the financial district.

★ ★

Since the parade was unplanned, no one had brought confetti. But stockbrokers in offices high above Broadway showered the crowds in ticker tape.

Since 1886, hundreds of Ticker-Tape Parades have wound their way through the Canyon of Heroes—the stretch of Broadway from Bowling Green to City Hall Park—celebrating major space missions and sports triumphs. Ticker tape is long gone, so office workers are now supposed to throw shredded documents out the window. But apparently, some can't be bothered to use the shredder.

The city now distributes confetti to staunch the risk of identity theft. Still, I'd hesitate before hiring a broker whose office overlooks that stretch of Broadway.

And Then There Were None
The New York Stock Exchange (NYSE)

On May 17, 1792, under a buttonwood tree at 68 Wall Street, twenty-four stockbrokers signed a pledge to trade only with each other. This "Buttonwood Agreement" laid the groundwork for what would later become the New York Stock Exchange.

In 1793 the twenty-four traders moved into the Tontine Coffee House on the northwest corner of Wall and Water Streets. Stock trading was frighteningly unregulated in those days. The Tontine was named after a capital-raising scheme that was once quite common in the United States and Europe: Each investor put a sum of money into a tontine and received annual dividends on this investment. When an investor died, his or her share would be redistributed among the survivors. Sound like a recipe for murder? No surprise—the tontine has inspired countless thrillers.

Though none of the twenty-four Buttonwood brokers offed each other, the Tontine Coffee House was raucous. Violence and political protests erupted. Fistfights broke out every day following the French Revolution.

In 1922 the NYSE moved to its current site at 18 Broad Street.

Now that you know the NYSE's shifty history, why not
visit the spooky facade at night?

★ ★

Today, most trading takes place on computer screens. Tontines have long been illegal, though they were replaced by less obvious, more insidious dangers, like the credit default swaps that helped bring the world economy to its knees in 2008.

While most stockbrokers are far more interested in making a killing than in killing anyone, the NYSE trading floor remains rowdy. Every weekday morning, the opening bell rings, and brokers face off on the trading floor.

The visitors' gallery has been closed to the public since 9/11. But if you're lucky, you'll get invited to a private event with a cocktail reception on the trading floor. There you can nosh on canapés amid the trading stations and spill your saketini on one of the thousands of tickers and monitors.

Chinatown Tunnel: From Secret Labyrinth to Underground Strip Mall
Wing Fat Shopping Arcade

In tales of Chinatown's tong warfare, ax-swinging Chinese gangsters stalk each other through narrow alleys then vanish into subterranean tunnels the instant the cops appear.

These underground labyrinths may be more than mythical. From the 1880s until the 1930s, the On Leong and Hip Sing tongs battled in the streets of Manhattan's Chinatown. One famous getaway involved a shootout on August 6, 1905. Tom Lee, the leader of the On Leong tong, was enjoying a night at the old Chinese Opera House at 5 Doyers Street, when the rival tong stood up and emptied its .44s on Tom and his gang. The On Leong fired back, but when the cops finally clubbed their way through the smoke and rioting crowds, they found only four dead gangsters. Both tongs had disappeared, hauling their wounded into a secret tunnel under the old opera house.

Sensational as it seems, the mobsters probably did escape through a passageway in the cellar. You can still visit the main tunnel. At 15 Doyers Street, on an alley lined with hair salons, a staircase descends

Chinese gangsters made quick escapes through this
tunnel—now a fluorescently lit shopping arcade. ·

★ ★

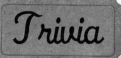

Trivia

NYC has been the most populous city since 1790.

into a basement hallway that snakes under what was once the Chinese Opera House and ends in the lobby of the Wing Fat Mansion at Chatham Square.

Once a harrowing escape route, the tunnel is now the benign Wing Fat Shopping Arcade, featuring acoustic ceiling tiles, fluorescent lights, and a hodgepodge of offices belonging to acupuncturists, philatelists, and Master Pun Yin, the Chinese metaphysician who feng shui'd the Trump International Tower. Along the way, one passes some locked doors with ominous KEEP OUT signs. Perhaps they lead to the labyrinth of tunnels that the police blocked off in the 1930s, after the tongs declared truce.

In any case, the Wing Fat Shopping Arcade is a consummate example of the New York drive to make every inch of space into commercial real estate. Even an underground gangster getaway is now a strip mall.

Find the not-so-secret entrance to Wing Fat at 15 Doyers Street.

An Island
for a Dollar

Governor's Island, half a mile south of Manhattan, belonged to the federal government until January 3, 2003, when then President George W. Bush sold 87 percent of the island to New York State for $1. Heck of a deal, Georgie.

* *

From Freshwater to Sewage

Foley Square

Manhattan's Civic Center, Foley Square, was built on the best sewage swamp money could buy.

Stand in the square bordered by Worth, Lafayette, Centre, and Duane Streets, and look south to where Federal Plaza dovetails in Centre Street. The skyscrapers along the southern tip of the square define the edge of what was once a 48-acre, 60-foot-deep freshwater lake in Lower Manhattan.

This lake spanned north to present-day Canal Street and east to what is now Mulberry. The Lenape fished in it. The Dutch, who skated on it in the winter, called it Kalch-Hook or Kalk, meaning "chalk" or "lime." From the early 1600s to 1812, slaves imported from Africa buried as many as 15,000 to 20,000 of their dead along the shores of the lake. (The monument at the center of the square commemorates the African-American Burial Ground.)

When the English seized New Amsterdam in 1664, they bastard-ized the name Kalch to Collect. They also brought industry to Man-hattan and allowed the tanneries and slaughterhouses to dump their waste into Collect Pond, the city's supply of fresh drinking water. By 1800, according to some accounts, Collect Pond was "a very sink and common sewer" with piles of trash rising fifteen feet above water level.

In 1805, after a few typhoid and cholera outbreaks, local authorities drained the polluted water by opening a forty-foot-wide canal—now known as Canal Street, NYC's most highly trafficked thoroughfare. They then shoveled dirt from a nearby hill into Collect Pond, but this only created a foul-smelling swamp.

An early nineteenth-century white flight ensued. As wealthy Brits fled the region, land prices plummeted, and Joseph Astor and other real estate speculators came in for the kill. They bought up the swamp, built rickety tenements on top of sewage, and charged newly arrived immigrants unconscionable rents.

"Doing the slums" from *Frank Leslie's Illustrated Newspaper*, 1885
LIBRARY OF CONGRESS

Nineteenth-century Manhattan welcomed immigrants—largely because the industrialists loved an endless supply of cheap labor. In the 1820s, as Irish immigrants and free blacks crammed into the tenements, the unimaginably destitute slum of Five Points took shape on what had once been Collect Pond.

Ironically, Five Points was also the city's main tourist attraction. The rich went there to see poverty and despair beyond anything they could imagine.

★ ★

What—and Where—was Five Points?

Intersection of Baxter and Worth

Aside from one or two sordid areas of London, mid-nineteenth-century Five Points (also known as the Sixth Ward) was the most overcrowded place in the world. Immigrants, settling in tenements with no running water, no toilets, and no sewage system, made such meager wages that they had to take in whole families of boarders just to make rent. In the 1850s, the population density of the Sixth Ward reached 310.4 people per acre. Five people were crammed into the average two-room apartment, but 46 percent of these dwellings housed six

I'm standing at the former site of Five Points, now covered with concrete and municipal buildings.
BOBBY MORGAN

★ ★

or more, and 17 percent held eight or more people. (In the 1920s, Harlem had a population density of over 215,000 per square mile, or thirty four people per acre—only one-tenth the density of Five Points.)

Today, it's hard to find where Five Points used to be. Between 1885 and 1895, municipal authorities razed Five Points to the ground. They truncated and renamed the streets and blanketed much of the intersection with parks and buildings. (This only displaced the tenement dwellers into even more overcrowded apartments on the Lower East Side.)

From the 1820s to the 1890s, Five Points lay at the intersection of three streets: Orange (now Baxter) Street, Cross (now Mosco) Street, and Anthony (now Worth) Street. Orange and Cross Streets bisected each other. This would have created a regular four-cornered intersection, but the third street, Anthony, bisected the northern quadrant and ended at the junction—creating five corners, or "points."

Chinatown's main park, Columbus Park, lies between Mosco and the intersection of Baxter and Worth. All that remains is the three-way intersection where Baxter meets Worth Street.

To find Five Points, stand at the intersection of Baxter and Worth,

Horse Pee
In the mid-1800s, horses discharged sixty thousand gallons of urine into the streets of Manhattan every day. Horses were the main form of transportation, and a single horse excreted a daily average of two gallons of urine and forty-five pounds of manure. People walked through rivers of horse urine. In the streets of Five Points, pigs ran wild, eating the horse feces.

drink a pint of cheap whisky, roll around in the gutter, imagine drunks staggering through the streets, prostitutes coming on to customers, pigs running wild, and fights breaking out—all amid crumbling tenements, reeking sewage, and gunfire.

A Black Man in Black Face
William Henry Lane (Master Juba)

After New York abolished slavery in 1827, former slaves settled near Five Points along Cow Bay, the "African Quarter." Cow Bay was deemed the city's most scandalous street, because it was the only place where one could see a white woman in a black man's arms. This also meant that cultures melded and spawned new art forms.

When Charles Dickens visited NYC in 1842, he was thoroughly unimpressed with everything he saw, except for a dance contest at Almack's Dance Hall—situated near the present-day site of Columbus Park Pavilion. The judges measured the dancers' speed by counting stomps. A black dancer named William Henry Lane, known as Master Juba, combined elements of the walkaround (a plantation slave step) with the Irish jig in a lightning-fast percussive dance. Some historians claim he invented tap-dancing.

Lane was one of the only black performers to appear in white theaters in the 1840s—at a time when most theaters banned nonwhites. Unfazed, P. T. Barnum put Juba in blackface and a wooly wig and set him onstage at the prestigious Vauxhall Gardens. Juba—*a black man disguised as a white man pretending to be black*—outdanced all the white minstrels.

Today, Columbus Park Pavilion stands near the former site of Almack's Dance Hall. In the 1890s Columbus Park was built over the charred remains of the Mulberry Bend slum. Calvert Vaux, who co-designed Manhattan's Central Park and Brooklyn's Prospect Park, also planned Columbus Park—to add trees and grass to one of Manhattan's oldest and most depressed residential neighborhoods. The area has been home to successive waves of immigrants—first German

★ ★

Jews, then Irish, then southern Italians, and most recently Chinese.

When you visit Chinatown, spend some time in Columbus Park, bounded by Baxter, Worth, Bayard, and Mulberry Streets. On warm, sunny days, you'll see people of all ages, including older Chinese men carrying bamboo cages. They're taking their songbirds out for a stroll.

Columbus Park Pavilion, near the former site of Almack's, where Charles Dickens watched Master Juba dance.
BOBBY MORGAN

Prince of Humbugs
P. T. Barnum

When P. T. Barnum moved to NYC in 1834, he exhibited Joice Heth, a wizened African-American woman with long, twisted fingernails, who claimed she was the 161-year-old wet nurse of the infant George Washington. After she died, the autopsy showed she was only eighty, but Barnum had found his calling.

In 1842, he opened Barnum's American Museum on the southeast

P. T. Barnum didn't enter the circus business until age sixty-one, but by then he'd been marketing "human curiosities" for thirty years.
THE STROBRIDGE LITHO. CO., 1899

corner of Broadway and Ann. He crammed the five-story building with trained bears, elephants, snakes, a flea circus, Ned the learned seal, wax figures like Jefferson Davis in drag, the Feejee Mermaid (a fish tail sewn onto a mummified monkey), beluga whales cramped in a fifty-eight-foot tank, midgets like General Tom Thumb, giants like Anna Swan, the eponymous Siamese twins Chang and Eng Bunker, and countless other "freaks," whom Barnum displayed in a manner we'd find hideously offensive today.

But Barnum's American Museum was considered thoroughly respectable. Possibly the most popular attraction in the nineteenth-century United States, the museum occupied a place of honor directly south of City Hall and near the courthouse. This prime location gave Barnum a unique opportunity to comment on prominent legal cases. When Polly Bodine was on trial for murder in 1844, Barnum created "The Witch of Staten Island"—a wax diorama depicting Bodine as an old hag chopping up her niece and sister-in-law with a bloody ax. So much for the right to be presumed innocent until proven guilty.

Tour a virtual re-creation of Barnum's American Museum at www .lostmuseum.cuny.edu/home.html.

Naked Women Onstage—As Long as They Don't Move

In 1907, Broadway impresario Florenz "Flo" Ziegfeld launched the Follies, a wildly popular revue featuring lavish sets with as many as 120 women onstage at once. As an archaic law made it legal for a woman to be naked on stage if she didn't move, the Follies featured *tableaux vivants* with scantily clad women posing as well-known sculptures or figures from paintings. In one Alfred Stieglitz photo, Fanny Brice poses dishabille as Rodin's *Thinker*.

Caricaturing current events, Ziegfeld Girls flew over the audience in 1909 in a replica of a Wright Brothers airplane. After the United States joined World War I, the 1918 Follies opened with Kay Laurell—breast exposed—perched atop a globe, overlooking trenches, gunfire, and a dying soldier.

★ ★

Disruptions were not uncommon. Starting in 1912, plants in the audience shouted at the performers onstage to get on with the show. During one show, Fanny Brice and another star, Lillian Lorraine, got into a screaming fight backstage. The row got so loud it interrupted the show, and—in a spontaneous fit of rage—Fanny dragged Lillian across the stage by her hair to the audience's wild applause.

Ziegfeld tried his hand at many shows
before his great success with the Follies.
This advertisement is from 1899.
THE STROBRIDGE LITHO. CO., 1899

21

2

Midtown Manhattan
(Fourteenth Street to Fifty-ninth Street)

Midtown Manhattan—epitome of urban chaos, home to Times Square, Rockefeller Center, the Empire State Building, the Chrysler Building, workplace for more than seven hundred thousand commuters. Roughly five square miles of madly coveted commercial space, this patch of real estate is constantly being reinvented, remade.

Midtown is a grid whose streets march north to south and east to west—or at least the street names suggest this. The map drawn up for the Commissioners' Plan of 1811 aligned the island so it looked like a finger pointing due north and mapped out a grid of east-west streets and north-south avenues. But any respectable map will show you that Manhattan tilts. Since the grid is rotated 28.9 degrees east of geographic north, Manhattan's avenues run northeast-by-north to southwest-by-south, while the numbered streets dart northwest-by-west to southeast-by-east.

To make life easier, everyone pretends Manhattan streets run north to south and east to west.

Everyone pretends, that is, except for Broadway.

One can't talk about Midtown without talking about Broadway. The brightest, most exalted street, Broadway is also the oldest, once a Native American trail. Midtown owes its rise as a global theater and commerce hub to Broadway's antics—its diagonal jaunt across Manhattan's middle. From Battery to Tenth Street, Broadway, like other avenues, heads northeast-by-north. Then at Tenth, it veers left and sprints diagonally across Midtown due north—as though it had decided to chase the North Star, no matter what all those conformist streets did.

Iconoclast on the Midtown grid, Broadway collides with other main drags, breaching a series of open plazas: Union Square, Madison Square at Fifth Avenue, Greeley and Herald Squares at Sixth, Times Square at Seventh, and Columbus Circle at Eighth. Historically, the squares south of Tenth were boxed in, enclosed on all sides by private homes, while the Midtown squares—sliced open by Broadway—offered wide-open spaces, bristling with public life, street theater, festivals, farmer's markets, demonstrations, and tourists looking to buy a local bridge.

★ ★

Teddy Bears

Theodore Roosevelt Birthplace

Teddy Roosevelt was the only U.S. president born in NYC—at 28 East Twentieth Street. The "birthplace" that stands there now is a reconstruction of the original brownstone, which was torn down. This is apt, because Roosevelt reinvented himself. As a young politician, he put people off with his effete manner, New York Brahmin accent, and aristocratic airs. In his mid-twenties, he hightailed it to the Dakotas to ranch and raise cattle—which was the best possible move for his political career. The public lapped up his newfound manliness and cowboy mystique.

Roosevelt was known as a big-game hunter. A year after he took office, the governor of Mississippi, Andrew Longino, invited him on a bear hunt. Pickings were slim. When three days passed with hardly a bear in sight, the governor apparently felt the need to avert a diplomatic crisis. His aides chased down an aged and infirm bear, tied it to a tree, and invited the president to fire. Roosevelt politely declined.

The incident made national news, and on November 16, 1902, the *Washington Post* ran a cartoon by Clifford Berryman showing the president refusing to shoot a baby bear—though the actual bear involved in the incident had been getting on in years. The cartoon was an instant hit. Berryman drew numerous versions, and a Brooklyn toymaker made a stuffed "Teddy Bear" in Teddy Roosevelt's honor.

The Theodore Roosevelt Birthplace has numerous Teddy Bear tokens on display, as well as period furnishings, Rough Rider photos, trophy animals Roosevelt shot and stuffed himself, political cartoons of Teddy the Trustbuster firing cannons at monopolies, even the shirt he was wearing when he was shot on his way to give a campaign speech. (The shirt must have been bleached hundreds of times to get the blood out.)

The bullet lodged in Roosevelt's right side, but his overcoat, metal spectacles case, and the fifty-page manuscript of his speech absorbed much of the force. Ignoring the pain, blood, and ruined manuscript,

Roosevelt delivered a ninety-minute, extemporaneous speech, before yielding to doctors' pleas for hospitalization. "I did not care a rap for being shot," he said later. "It is a trade risk, which every prominent public man ought to accept as a matter of course."

See these Roosevelt relics for yourself at 28 East Twentieth Street between 9:00 a.m. and 5:00 p.m., Tuesday through Saturday, or online at www.nps.gov/thrb.

A series of Clifford Berryman cartoons inspired the Teddy Bear.

Reverend Billy and the Church of Life After Shopping

Reverend Billy (William Talen) got his start as a street theater preacher in Times Square "saving souls from the fiery abyss of shopping." Now, joined by the thirty-five-member Life After Shopping Gospel Choir, he can often be found in Starbucks, Wal-Mart, Disney, and other chain stores laying hands upon cash registers to exorcise the demons of consumer culture and corporate greed. The reverend and choir also appear at numerous events and have taken their Shopocalypse Tour across the United States and United Kingdom.

Since it's not possible to cease purchasing completely, Reverend Billy urges consumers to put money into their communities by buying from local independent stores rather than chain stores and purchasing products that don't harm the environment.

Reverend Billy and the Church of Life After Shopping march in the NYC Halloween parade during their Sidamo Prayer Campaign against Starbucks.
FRED ASKEW PHOTOGRAPHY

The title of his manifesto—*What should I do if Reverend Billy is in my store?*—comes from a Starbucks worker's memo, but Reverend Billy takes pains not to antagonize employees, so you don't have to fear him if you work in Starbucks—only if you own Starbucks. www.RevBilly.com

✦ ✦

Trivia

In NYC, it is a crime to throw pig slop into the street.

Scintillation Central

Times Square

Times Square's towering digital advertisements, bright lights, and endlessly milling crowds have long symbolized the distilled essence of New York City: desire—restless, unhinged, insatiable in its quest for ever newer, flashier titillation. The "Crossroads of the World" may seem too iconic to be a curiosity, but its transformations are truly bizarre.

In the 1890s, so-called Longacre Square was a horse-trading center and red-light district, until 1899, when Oscar Hammerstein I built the theaters that turned it into the vaudeville capital of the world. With this surge of construction, Longacre got a new name: Times Square, after the Times Building was completed in 1904.

By 1930, Broadway's Golden Age had ended, and by the 1970s, Forty-Second Street had devolved into "The Deuce," a byword for seedy urban decay. For several decades, politicians and urban developers sparred over urban renewal plans. In 1993, they offered Forty-Second Street to the Walt Disney Company. But Disney preferred suburban settings for its private, hermetically controlled, child-safe theme parks (secretly known to their employees as Mauswitz), so Disney's first impulse was to put a gate around Forty-Second Street—to make a Garden of Eden for cartoon characters and middle-class families, with the smut and riffraff of The Deuce fenced out. This wasn't feasible, since half of New Jersey passes through Forty-Second Street every day on their way to work. (The other half has better sense.)

In the mid-1990s, former mayor Rudolph Giuliani finally carried off the highly controversial gentrification—also known as the

★ ★

Nobel Laureate economist Paul Krugman quipped about Times Square, "No one goes there anyway. It's too crowded."

Disneyfication—of Times Square. But, as multinational corporations supplanted hustlers, porn shops, and grindhouses with clean, well-lighted family fun, countless New Yorkers waxed nostalgic for the old, bawdy Times Square. Ironically, the Crossroads of the World is a victim of its own success. By spawning the pop culture industry and exporting the likes of Disney around the globe, Times Square has turned commercial hubs worldwide into Times Square lookalikes. So Times Square resembles every other bustling commercial district—just busier and much more packed with people.

Times Square spans the intersection of Broadway and Seventh Avenue from West Forty-Second to West Forty-Seventh Street. It's open 24-7 year-round.

Patience and Fortitude

New Yorkers are very devoted to Patience and Fortitude, the stone lions guarding the main branch of the New York Public Library on Fifth Avenue at Forty-Second Street. In the 1930s, Mayor Fiorello La Guardia named them after the qualities New Yorkers needed to survive the Great Depression. Before that, the lions were called Lord and Lady Astor, though both are obviously male.

Fortitude—plainly a male lion—was once known as Lady Astor.

★ ★

The Naked Cowboy

Times Square is exhibitionist central. Unless you happen to be a
40-by-40-foot animated digital billboard, you have to be truly unique
to get noticed. Yet, some average-size mortals succeed. For more
than ten years, Robert Burck has sung and strummed his guitar on
the streets of Times Square in nothing but western boots, a 10-gallon
hat, and tighty-whities—with the words Naked Cowboy emblazoned
on his butt. While he's not exactly nude, "Cowboy in Dishabille" isn't
half as catchy, and he's about as bare as one can get in public without being busted.

This skivvy-clad busker may seem inimitable, especially in sub-zero
temperatures. But in early 2008, one of those huge digital billboards
in Times Square actually tried. On the M&M digital display, an animated blue M&M appeared—nearly naked (if it's possible for an
M&M to be naked), plucking a guitar and wearing cowboy boots, hat,
and briefs. Burck sued Mars Inc. for stealing his trademark look, and
the two parties reached an undisclosed settlement in a case that one
judge dubbed "the Naked Cowboy versus the Blue M&M."

Burck soon made news again. In July 2009, he announced his
candidacy for mayor against then incumbent Michael Bloomberg,
because "no one's done more with less." The street performer
dropped out of the race, but New Yorkers appreciated his platform of
"bringing transparency to a whole new level."

Time-Travel Square

One June night in 1950 in Times Square, a man materialized out of
nowhere dressed like a Victorian gentleman with mutton-chop whis-
kers, a high silk hat, and cutaway coat. Gawking at the cars and signs
as if he'd never seen them before, he stumbled into the street, and a
taxi struck and killed him instantly.

Searching for clues to the man's identity, police found a letter
postmarked 1876 and business cards with the name Rudolph Fentz.

* *

Trivia

An NYC ordinance prohibits a woman from wearing "body-hugging clothing" on the street. But if you're worried that your shirt is too tight, simply take it off. A different law stipulates that a woman may go topless as long she isn't using her bare breasts "for business purposes."

They found Rudolph Fentz Jr. in an old phone book and spoke to his widow. The woman said that her husband's father had vanished in 1876 and was never heard from again. A missing persons report filed in 1876 confirmed her story.

This tale circulated among paranormal researchers as evidence of time travel, until folklorist and UFO investigator Chris Aubeck traced it back through time and discovered it was originally a science-fiction piece, "I'm Scared," authored by Jack Finney and published in *Collier's* in 1951. In 1953, a writer eager to prove time travel reprinted the story without permission and didn't mention it was fiction. For half a century, time travel enthusiasts treated the sci-fi tale as fact.

Dragonslayer and an Anatomically Correct Elephant

U.N. Sculpture Garden, First Avenue at Forty-Seventh Street

The United Nations can't say no to art. Imagine you started an organization to promote peace and dialogue in your neighborhood. Soon your grateful neighbors were bringing "gifts" to decorate your lawn. Once you let one neighbor install the bird feeder she built with her own hands, it would be hard to turn down her rival's neon-pink lawn flamingo.

In 1985, the U.N. tried to implement a policy of refusing new art

★ ★

offerings. Member nations had donated so much art that the U.N. grounds were strewn with mediocre works from well-meaning governments. But the new policy didn't last long. It's hard to say no when the stakes are world peace.

The U.N. couldn't refuse a 40-foot statue of Saint George the Dragonslayer plunging a cruciform spear into a dragon made from salami slices of Soviet SS-20 and U.S. Pershing nuclear warheads. The USSR presented this gift to commemorate the 1988 U.S.–Soviet accord to destroy intermediate and short-range nukes. But the

Saint George usually impales a dragon, but during recent construction, he was impaling a row of trash dumpsters instead.

sculpture has sparked controversy. How could the U.N.—an international organization with no religious creed—give such a privileged spot to a Christian icon? (In fact, why would the USSR donate a Christian icon in the first place?)

The elephant sculpture was problematic for entirely different reasons. In 1998, the governments of Kenya, Namibia, and Nepal presented the U.N. with a statue of an African Bull Elephant, complete with an anatomically correct member. The artist had made the piece by tranquilizing a live elephant and casting him in bronze. Supposedly the model worked for peanuts. The organ drew so much attention that the U.N. surrounded the statue with a hedge of bushes. Fig leaves plainly wouldn't suffice.

The audience tittered during the dedication ceremony, as U.N. Secretary General Kofi Annan—apparently referring to the work as a whole—proclaimed, "The sheer size of the creature humbles us. As well it should, for it tells us that some things are bigger than we are."

Is There Sex Life After Death?
Belasco Theater

Broadway impresario David Belasco made his home directly above his Belasco Theater. His lavish ten-room suite featured an infamous casting couch, where he "interviewed" actresses for parts in his shows. Belasco always wore a cleric's collar and a robe—a strange costume for a showman, let alone a ladies' man.

Belasco died in 1931, but evidently never moved out. The impresario's ghost not only haunts the theater, but—as Tom Meyers remarked on the Bowery Boys podcast—he's also "one of the most reliable shows on Broadway." Most sightings take place when an actor onstage peers into the upper balcony and sees a figure in a black robe sitting alone.

This revenant—affectionately dubbed the Monk, due to his cleric's garb—has also been known to come onstage and offer acting advice. Actors generally consider this a good omen, except when the

The ghost of Broadway impresario David Belasco supposedly haunts
the Belasco Theater and pats actresses on the butt.

ghost—still philandering in the afterlife—pats an actress on the rump. (One wonders, do ghosts have genitals?)

Some say the Monk is haunted by a female ghost, perhaps a jilted lover. She's called the Blue Lady. This is a common name for she-ghosts. I don't know why, but I can assure you she's not the *Green* Lady in the New York Harbor. Once an entire casting crew overheard a loud fight between a man and a woman that seemed to be coming from behind Belasco's portrait, but when the crew ventured into the next room to see what was going on, no one was there.

I've heard the Belasco Theater on 111 West Forty-Fourth Street is worth seeing, but it was under construction while I was writing this book. The Schubert Organization also informed me that they don't allow visitors into any of their theaters without tickets. Perhaps they're trying to keep the ghostbusters out.

Best *New York* Post Headlines

The *New York Post* has won awards for hilarious headlines. Some of the best:

- **Headless Body in Topless Bar (1982)**
- **Bad Heir Day (Brooke Astor's son indicted on charges of larceny, 2007)**
- **"I Am Death Wish Vigilante" (Bernie Goetz turns himself in, 1985)**
- **Amy's Nude Romps in Jail (1993)**
- **Kiss Your Asteroid Goodbye! (Meteor misses Earth, 1998)**

★ ★

Darger's Genius

The Henry Darger Study Center at the American Folk Art Museum

Henry Darger, a recluse and retired janitor, told no one about his magnum opus, *The Story of the Vivian Girls, in What Is Known as the Realms of the Unreal, of the Glandeco-Angelinnian War Storm, Caused by the Child Slave Rebellion* (*Realms* for short). The idea had come to him when he was nineteen—shortly after he'd escaped from an institute for so-called "feeble-minded" children—and he'd been writing the novel ever since. By the time Darger reached age eighty-one, *Realms* consisted of fifteen thousand, single-spaced, doubled-sided pages and over three hundred illustrations, which show the seven Vivian sisters leading a revolt on a distant planet to free children from slavery.

Darger penned other works, too—his ten-thousand-page, handwritten *Crazy House* and *The History of My Life*, which begins with two hundred pages of autobiography, then turns into a five-thousand-page fiction about a tornado named Sweetie Pie.

Weather, for Darger, was a serious moral matter. For ten years, he faithfully recorded the daily weather forecast, the actual conditions, and a painstaking ethical analysis of how well the weatherman was performing the duties of his office.

In 1973, as Darger lay dying, his landlords, Nathan and Kiyoko Lerner, entered his tiny one-room apartment in Chicago and found the four manuscripts totaling thirty thousand pages. Nathan Lerner, a photographer, spotted the illustrations of the Vivian Girls and recognized talent.

Sadly, Darger didn't live to hear of his own fame. He is now deemed one of the most remarkable self-taught artists of the twentieth century. The American Folk Art Museum houses the largest public collection of his works, including the paintings for which he is best known.

Visit the museum at 45 West Fifty-Third Street Tuesday through Sunday from 10:30 a.m. to 5:30 p.m., Friday from 11:30 a.m. to 7:30 p.m., or on the Web at www.folkartmuseum.org.

Blood, Gore, and a Unique Dining Experience
The Jekyll and Hyde Club

We humans like our food dead, as opposed to kicking and screaming, but we want those preparing our dinner to be alive. Picky, picky.

Despite an overwhelming number of cadaverous employees, the Jekyll and Hyde Club remains one of NYC's favorite theme

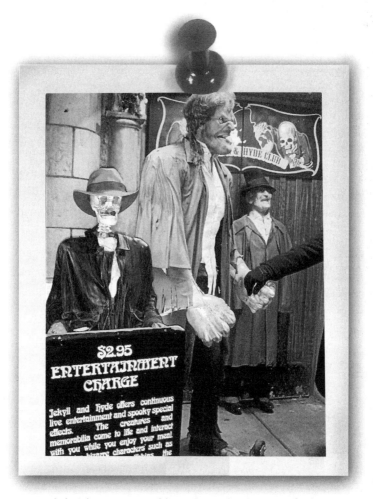

Don't let those arms and legs simmering in stews fool you.
The Jekyll and Hyde Club is strictly noncannibalistic.

restaurants. Their secret? The "deceased"—a mixture of humans and robots—regularly bounce back to life so you can chow down at Chuck E. Cheese for the goth and Halloween set.

Maxmillian Gorey, the bartender killed in a blender accident, awakes in a state of advanced decomposition. The werewolf, Tobias Bloodworth, talks, though his head is stuffed and mounted on the wall. A wolf in Sheetrock's clothing.

In addition to the necrotic dining, you're invited to tour the restaurant's four floors, participate in a séance, mad science experiments, and other English Gothic pastimes. The restaurant is most popular among kids and tourists, since the acts get repetitive after the first time, and—while the food doesn't usually bite back—it isn't tasty enough to entice locals.

Nonetheless, most restaurant-goers agree that the Jekyll and Hyde Club surpasses its rival theme restaurant, Mars 2112, which features a space trip to Mars (with a bad video), dirty bathrooms, and aliens who would really rather be elsewhere.

Jekyll and Hyde would be delighted to have you for dinner anytime between 11:30 a.m. and 11:30 p.m. Sunday through Thursday, or between 11:30 a.m. and 12:30 a.m. Friday and Saturday. Pay them a visit at 1409 Avenue of the Americas, or on the web at www.jekyll andhydeclub.com.

3

Uptown West Manhattan
(North of Fifty-ninth Street, West of Fifth Avenue)

Uptown West covers *a wide, largely residential swath of Manhattan from the Hudson River to Fifth Avenue and from West Fifty-Ninth Street to West 220th Street and Inwood Hill Park. This region is home to Columbia University, Barnard College, the affluent Upper West Side, and perhaps most famously Harlem.*

Harlem's cultural output did not stop in the 1920s with the Black cultural explosion known as the Harlem Renaissance. In more recent decades, Harlem has been a major player in hip-hop music. We'll return to hip-hop in Chapter 7, since most hip-hop historians say the genre emerged in the Bronx. But if you're a fan, don't miss the Harlem/Bronx: Birthplace of Hip Hop Tour, courtesy of Hush Tours (www.hushtours .com). On these bus tours, celebrated emcees introduce you to landmarks, spin early rap records, and give you their firsthand account of hip-hop history.

If you see NYC as synonymous with Downtown or Midtown, Harlem (from roughly 110th to 155th Street on the West Side) is probably farther uptown than you've ever dreamed of going. But I suggest you venture even farther—to Manhattan's northernmost shore. In Inwood Hill Park—the only part of the island largely untouched by wars and development—you can see ridges and caves that were hollowed out roughly fifty thousand years ago when thousand-foot-high glaciers covered and crushed the region. The Lenape Indians used these caves for shelter. For more than sixty centuries, they hunted and fished on the banks of a

★ ★

Inwood Hill Park. I snapped this photo looking out from inside a cave that the Lenape may have used for shelter.

tidal strait that separated Manna-hata ("the island of many hills") from the mainland. They called the region Shorakapok ("the place between the ridges" or "the sitting down place") before the Dutch renamed the strait Spuyten Duyvil.

A huge varsity letter C, which the Columbia crew team painted on the Bronx side of Spuyten Duyvil Creek, now marks the main site where the Lenape camped. Needless to say, the C stands for Columbia, not camp or cave.

The Eruv

In early 2010, a series of blizzards wreaked havoc for NYC Jews who observe traditional Judaic law around the Sabbath. The storm broke the translucent fish wire, strung from lamppost to lamppost, that marks the boundaries of the Upper West Side eruv.

Traditional Judaic law forbids one to carry anything outside one's home on the Sabbath. An eruv (pronounced air-uv) is a ritual borderline that extends the boundaries of the home so that Orthodox Jews can carry as long as they remain within the eruv. But when the wire breaks, they can't tote prayer books, food, or tissues, or even push baby strollers outside their homes.

In 1905, the Hasidic community on the old Lower East Side used the Third Avenue elevated train and the East River as markers for one of the first eruvim in North America. The present-day Manhattan eruv started on the Upper West Side in 1994; in 2004, it was extended to the East River. For thirteen years, the eruv reached no farther south than the West or East Fifties. But in 2007, it was extended southward on the East Side to Houston Street between First and Sixth Avenues. Now there's talk of extending it westward to include Chelsea, Greenwich Village, the West Village, and the Meatpacking District.

But expanding the eruv isn't easy or cheap. It requires consultations with Talmudic scholars who specialize in urban eruvim, weekly inspections, and the complicated process of climbing ladders and stringing fish wire high up on telephone poles.

Noticeably, the eruv doesn't extend south of Houston. Even though the Lower East Side once had the world's largest Jewish community, the powerful Rabbi Moshe Feinstein believed that Manhattan traffic patterns and street layout did not permit an eruv. "Rav Moshe" died in 1986, but the majority of Lower East Side rabbis still defer to his word on Jewish law. Consequently, many Orthodox Jews have left the Lower East Side so they can carry on the Sabbath.

For centuries, Talmudic scholars have debated whether Manhattan Island itself is an eruv, since the surrounding water is deep enough

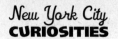

to be considered a wall. But for now, fish wire is strung along light poles, according to strict guidelines. If you look hard enough, you just might see it.

The eruv currently spans the width of Manhattan from Riverside Park to FDR Drive. On the West Side, it extends from West Fifty-Sixth to West 126th Street, and on the East Side from Houston Street to East 111th Street.

Churchgoing Elephants

If you're in NYC in October, don't miss the annual Blessing of the Animals at St. John the Divine, the cathedral of the Episcopal Diocese of New York. Most people bring their house pets to be blessed, but if you're lucky, you'll see a horse, a camel—even an elephant—lumber through the wide-open Portal of Paradise. The elephant comes for the blessing each year.

St. John the Divine is the world's largest Gothic cathedral, but it began with a Byzantine-Romanesque design in 1892. Construction has been under way ever since—for the last 120 years. In 1909, the trustees decided to switch from Byzantine-Romanesque to Gothic design, so they hired a Gothic Revival architect to "Gothicize" what had already been built.

The cathedral was named after John of Patmos, author of the Book of Revelation. This New Testament book is heavy on numerology, especially the number seven—seven seals, seven trumpets, seven plagues. Consequently, the cathedral's design privileges the number seven. The entire cathedral is 601 (6 + 0 + 1 = 7) feet in length, the nave ceiling reaches 124 (1 + 2 + 4 = 7) feet high, and seven chapels radiate from the end of the choir.

Visit St. John the Divine at 1047 Amsterdam Avenue at West 112th Street Monday through Saturday from 7:00 a.m. to 6:00 p.m., Sunday from 7:00 a.m. to 7:00 p.m., or online at www.StJohnDivine.org. To learn about its fascinating construction, take the Vertical Tour up the spiral stone staircase.

Homezooing

My six-pound housecat likes to look out the window. So did Ming, the 400-pound Bengal-Siberian tiger that Antoine Yates raised as a pet in his fifth-floor Harlem apartment. In 2003, the front page of the *New York Daily News* featured Ming growling out the window at the policeman who'd scaled the building to investigate.

Though Yates had taken excellent care of his pet, his mother had moved out recently because she was scared of the tiger. At the time of his arrest, Yates lived with Ming and Al, a 5½–foot caiman alligator. The tiger and caiman each had its own bedroom.

Neoclassical Architecture Meets Hippie Community Art
General Grant National Memorial

In the 1950s, Grant's Tomb was the butt of a Groucho Marx joke on the radio quiz show *You Bet Your Life*. When a contestant botched every answer, Groucho would offer a question he couldn't miss: "Who's buried in Grant's Tomb?" "Grant" was an acceptable answer. "Grant and his wife, Julia" was even better. But technically, no one is *buried* in Grant's tomb, because it's a mausoleum. The coffins are above ground.

Overlooking the Hudson River, Grant's Tomb squats on its columns in grandiose splendor—the largest mausoleum in North America and one of the most ostentatious structures ever built in NYC. The architect, John Hemenway Duncan, was rather ambitious, to say the least: He was aiming for a cross between Napoleon's tomb and the Mausoleum at Halicarnassus, one of the Seven Wonders of the Ancient World.

Grant's Tomb was completed in 1897 but fell into disrepair during NYC's mid-twentieth-century financial crisis. By 1970, layers of graffiti covered its surface. People were shooting up and turning tricks, littering the plaza with plastic baggies, crack vials, and used condoms. One particularly enterprising vandal blew the beak off one of the stone eagles guarding the entrance. Never had a presidential monument sunk so low.

Apparently, the mound of ailing classical revivalism needed a dose of whimsy. In 1972, the National Parks Service hired sculptor Pedro Silva and architect Philip Danzig to create a community arts project. With CITYarts sponsorship, they designed the Rolling Bench,

The Rolling Bench rears up like a cobra with the columns of Grant's tomb in the background.

* *

Trivia

The so-called potty-parity law of 2005 reduced lines at the ladies' room by requiring all bars, cinemas, and other venues to have a two-to-one ratio of women's toilets to men's toilets.

a multicolor mosaic sculpture that snakes, twists, and loops in a semi-circle around three sides of Grant's Tomb. Kids who liked art and adults from eighteen to eighty-five made the mosaics, depicting people of all races, aquatic scenes, dancers, children, trees, taxicabs, cityscapes, castles, dragons, chessboards, dinosaurs. At four points, the sculpture rears up like a cobra and assumes a human face.

I'm a fan of the Rolling Bench, but I have to admit, this fine specimen of 1970s hippie art clashes a bit with the neoclassical gravitas of Grant's Tomb. I'd be hard-pressed to find two more disparate styles—except in Christ Community United Church, which I'll get to later in this chapter.

Located at Riverside Drive and 122nd Street, Grant's Tomb is open daily from 9:00 a.m. to 5:00 p.m. Find the monument online at www.nps.gov/gegr.

A Great Poker Hand—Minus Monarchy

Morris-Jumel Mansion

Manhattan's oldest freestanding house, the Morris-Jumel Mansion, once had a great poker hand, American style—with four presidents, instead of kings. On July 10, 1790, President Washington dined there with members of his cabinet, including future presidents John Adams, Thomas Jefferson, and John Quincy Adams.

In 1765, British colonel Roger Morris—son of architect Roger Morris—built the classical Georgian-style mansion as a summer home

Eliza Jumel claimed her bed once belonged to Napoleon.

on a 130-acre estate spanning the width of Manhattan Island from 155th to 168th Streets. One of Colonel Morris's claims to fame was that his wife, Mary Philipse, chose him over a little-known suitor named George Washington.

Twenty years later, the Morrises, who were Tories, hightailed it back to Britain. Washington, then commander-in-chief of the Continental Army, made their vacant mansion his headquarters in the fall of 1776.

Even with this illustrious cast, the most colorful person to occupy the mansion was Eliza Jumel. The house contains many of her furnishings, and some claim she's still around, too. I'm skeptical of ghosts, but if anyone were to haunt a house, she seems like the type.

Born into poverty, Eliza Bowen became the mistress then wife of Stephen Jumel, a French wine merchant who bought the property in 1810. While living in Paris in 1815, she apparently made the acquaintance of Napoleon Bonaparte and brought his bed and chandelier home to decorate her mansion. While there's no evidence that these items belonged to Napoleon, this is less far-fetched than Eliza's

"God, Harlem, USA"

Harlem has been teeming with churches since the first mass wave of black settlers in the early 1900s. According to Harlem Heritage Tours (www.harlemheritage.com), more than four hundred houses of worship, including many little "storefront churches," serve African Methodist Episcopalians, Baptists, Black Jews, Methodists, Mormons, Nation of Islam and other Black Muslim groups, Roman Catholics, Seventh Day Adventists, and a wide range of other religions, spiritual traditions, and denominations.

Many of Harlem's spiritual leaders are quite traditional, but there are exceptions—like the charismatic Reverend Major Jealous Divine. Born George Baker in 1879, "Father Divine" chose the middle name Jealous because the God of the Old Testament was a "jealous God." Though some have seen him as a forerunner of the Civil Rights movement, Father Divine insisted he wasn't black, forbade his followers to refer to themselves as members of any race, and—most controversially—claimed he was God. He nonetheless attracted such a large international following that the United States Postal Service delivered a letter addressed simply to "God, Harlem, USA" directly to his door.

claims that she was the illegitimate daughter of Napoleon or George Washington.

In 1832, Stephen Jumel fell on a pitchfork, and Eliza was accused of loosening his bandages and leaving him to bleed to death, though this was never proven. A year later, Eliza married former vice president Aaron Burr. He supposedly married her for her money, while she wed him for his reputation. The union was tumultuous and short-lived.

After Burr's death, Eliza was increasingly isolated. New York high society frowned upon the Jumels because they were Catholic and perhaps because Eliza had once been Stephen Jumel's mistress. Eliza lived to age ninety and developed some rather odd habits, like keeping an armed garrison around the house and riding the grounds daily at the head of twenty men.

The Morris-Jumel Mansion at 65 Jumel Terrace is open Wednesday through Sunday from 10:00 a.m. to 4:00 p.m. and Monday and Tuesday by appointment only. Go to www.morrisjumel.org for more info.

Let's Go Byzantine-Rococo
United Palace Theater

United Palace Theater is a fine example of the "Byzantine-Romanesque-Indo-Hindu-Sino-Moorish-Persian-Eclectic-Rococo-Deco style," as David W. Dunlap writes in *On Broadway: A Journey Uptown Over Time*. Visitors marvel at elaborate carvings of Buddhas, elephants, and bodhisattvas—strange sights in a building that currently serves as a Christian church.

This delirious structure was the last of five "Wonder Theaters" that Loew's built between 1925 and 1930. At the time, theaters were vying for business by offering over-the-top decor. Architect Thomas W. Lamb borrowed from the Kailasa rock-cut shrine in India, the Wat Phra Kaew temple in Thailand, and the Alhambra in Spain. The outside of the building combines "muqarnas"—the "stalactite vaults" unique to Islamic architecture—with classical, Indian, and Mayan elements. The odd mix of anachronisms and vaguely Eastern motifs

The facade of United Palace Theater is bizarre, but it's nothing compared to the Indo-Rococo interior.

pandered to Westerners' fantasies of sampling the exotic Orient: Step right up and buy a ninety-minute trip to sixth-century Byzantium or tenth-century Al-Andalus—all for the price of one movie ticket.

Though Loew's 175th Street Theater first housed vaudeville shows, it soon became a deluxe cinema. As TV supplanted film, demand for a 3,353-seat movie house waned. But Loew's was destined for a higher (or at least more lucrative) calling.

The Wonder Theater caught the eye of Reverend Ike (Frederick J. Eikerenkoetter II), a pioneering black televangelist who drove a different Mercedes each day. In 1969, he bought the building and renamed it the Palace Cathedral, and renovated it with authentic Louis XV and Louis XVI rococo furnishings. Instead of fantasy flights to Constantinople, Reverend Ike promised "money up to your arm-pits, a roomful of money and there you are, just tossing around in it like a swimming pool."

Speaking of swimming pools, one wonders how they heat the place in the winter. The building occupies a full block of 175th Street, Broadway, 176th Street, and Wadsworth Avenue. Since the late 1980s, the church has offset operating costs by renting out the Palace Auditorium for concerts and community events at a fraction of

Reverend Ike

"The Bible says Jesus rode on a borrowed ass. But I would rather ride in a Rolls-Royce than to ride somebody's ass," said Rev. Frederick J. Eikerenkoetter II, better known as Reverend Ike.

In the tradition of black spiritual leaders like Father Divine, Sweet Daddy Grace, and more recently Creflo Dollar, Reverend Ike preached a get-rich gospel. Saint Paul got it wrong: The love of money wasn't the root of evil; the *lack* of money was. But this didn't mean the haves should help the have-nots: "The best thing you can do for the poor," he preached, "is not be one of them." But while he called himself "the first black man in America to preach positive self-image psychology to the black masses within a church setting," other ministers and civil rights leaders claimed that he exploited urban blacks and ignored issues of social justice.

The one who prospered most from his gospel was Reverend Ike. "My garages runneth over," he often said, eying his mink-lined Rolls-Royces.

midtown costs. First hosting bachata and salsa concerts, United Palace earned the nickname Latin Radio City Music Hall, but recent performers include the Smashing Pumpkins, Bob Dylan, Sonic Youth, Beck, Jackson Browne, and Björk.

United Palace, aka the Palace Cathedral, is located at 4140 Broadway. For a taste of the building's split personality, go to www.united palaceconcerts.com and www.revike.org/palace.asp.

Not Your Average Altar

Saint Frances Xavier Cabrini Shrine

The Cabrini Shrine is a house of worship, not the best place to visit in a rowdy or giggly mood. Besides, you'll probably enjoy the calm, even if you're not Catholic. (I'm not, and I did.)

Entering the shrine, you'll see a truly unusual altar—a glass case containing what looks like the preserved body of a nun. A notice in the hall explains: "In a crystal coffin under the main altar of this chapel, [sic] are the precious remains of Saint Frances Xavier Cabrini, her skeleton covered in wax."

Mother Cabrini, the patron saint of immigrants, was the first U.S. citizen to be canonized in 1946.

The notice also describes how a Roman Commission opened Mother Cabrini's casket in 1933 and found that her body had decayed. This is hardly surprising: She'd died in 1917. But since the Middle Ages, the Catholic Church has given special veneration to the "Incorruptibles"—saints whose bodies remain remarkably preserved long after their death. An intact cadaver was considered divine proof of saintliness. When clerics pronounced a corpse Incorruptible, the remains would be hermetically sealed in a glass coffin and displayed as an object of veneration. Some Incorruptibles look like skeletons covered in old leather or brown papier-mâché. Many of the Incorruptibles were preserved by natural processes, like alkaline groundwater seeping into a tomb and mummifying the cadaver. In other cases the body was secretly embalmed or the records were lost.

★ ★

Saint Frances Xavier Cabrini, looks like a
perfectly preserved corpse, but
she's covered in wax.

Mother Cabrini was never pronounced Incorruptible. As the notice
makes clear, she "was raised to the honors of the altar, not because
of the state of her body after death, but on account of the heroic virtue she practiced during life."

Nonetheless, her wax head and hands make her look intact from
a distance. This has apparently started rumors. (At the time of this
writing, Wikipedia lists her as one of the Incorruptibles, citing a 1977
book by Joan Carroll Cruz.)

The gift shop sells bits of fabric that have touched Mother Cabrini's
body. In a tiny museum next to the chapel, a glass case displays her
nightgowns, underwear, a check she signed, and a horridly large
spring from her dentures. (She'd have to be a saint not to complain
about that thing in her mouth.)

The shrine, located at 701 Fort Washington, is open daily from
9:00 a.m. to 4:30 p.m.

Head-Shaped Reliquaries for the Skulls of Women Saints
The Cloisters

To our twenty-first-century minds, the concerns of medieval Europeans often seem strange and humorous. With no scientific understand-
ing of digestion, medieval theologians wondered how it was possible
for a human to eat and absorb food every day without turning into
a loaf of bread or a leg of lamb. Medieval Christian theologians also
worried about the dead saints, whose physical remains were preserved as relics in cathedrals throughout Europe. If a saint's toenail
was in Paris and his foreskin in Rome, how would God resurrect the
saint's physical body at the Last Judgment? Would all the body parts,

In the early 1500s, these reliquaries held the skulls of women
saints, and they were carried in parades on feast days.

dispersed across Europe, suddenly fly up into the air and be miracu-
lously reassembled into one intact body?

The Cloisters, a branch of the Metropolitan Museum focused on
medieval art and architecture, will transport you back to twelfth- to
fifteenth-century Europe. The building looks like a monastery and is,
in fact, constructed from five medieval French monasteries.

Among nearly five thousand artworks, including the famous Uni-
corn Tapestries, there are some truly bizarre objects and stories. In
one room, three busts of women stand on an altar. Reading the
description, you'll learn that the busts were reliquaries (containers for
relics) that once housed the skulls of women saints.

Many of the paintings and sculptures depict a saint or an angel
with a vanquished demon underfoot. The text beside a pine carving
of Saint Margaret explains that this saint was thrown in prison for
refusing to marry the governor of Antioch. As Margaret clutched a
crucifix in her cell, Satan took the form of a dragon and swallowed
her whole. Using her crucifix as a knife, the wily Margaret sliced open
the dragon's stomach and freed herself.

The Cloisters, located at 99 Margaret Corbin Drive in Fort Tryon
Park, is open Tuesday through Sunday from 9:30 a.m. to 5:15 p.m.
From November through February, it closes at 4:45 p.m. Go to www
.metmuseum.org/cloisters for more info.

Manhattan for Sale
Shorakkopoch Rock

Shorakkopoch Rock is invariably covered in dog pee—perhaps a comment on the deal that was cut. This boulder supposedly marks the
site where Peter Minuit in 1624 purchased Manhattan for trinkets and
beads worth sixty guilders, or $24.

Though thousands of history books repeat this yarn, it's part hear-
say and part fiction. The only evidence is an offhand remark in a letter
that the Dutch "bought the island of Manhates from the Wild Men

★ ★

The Shorakkopoch Rock. Dogs find it irresistible.

for the value of sixty guilders." No one knows who made the deal, or where it took place.

In *Gotham,* Edwin G. Burrow and Mike Wallace note that the story is a classic tale of urbanites pulling one off on the yokels—or worse, a racist yarn about dazzling the savages with shiny baubles, swindling them into handing over what would later become the most valuable patch of dirt on Earth.

In 1902, two historians actually claimed that the Lenape got a good deal: If the Indians had only deposited their $24 in a savings account at 6 percent compound interest, it would have grown to over two hundred million. But don't trust any historian who assumes

★ ★

the existence of a Lenape Federal Savings and Loan. Even if the Lenape had had European-style banks, the Europeans who slaughtered Indians for their land would certainly have looted their bank accounts, too.

While the $24 deal is a yarn about a shakedown, the tale itself is a kind of scam that would trick us into believing that the Europeans "acquired" Manhattan through a business deal between parties who both understood that an island was a piece of property that could be owned, purchased, and sold. But the Lenape were unfamiliar with the European notion of private property. They believed land was held in trust for Kishelemukong, the Creator, and could not be owned or sold. Whatever occurred, they probably had no idea they were giving up the right to live on their island.

In fact, the story of the shady business deal covers a much uglier history: The Europeans seized Manhattan by conquest, not by business deals. But like the myth of Romulus and Remus founding Rome, the fiction gives New York City a sense of identity and purpose, even a shady kind of legitimacy. New York is a capital of capital, a city of dealmakers—even wheeler-dealers.

And by the way, want to buy a bridge?

Enter Inwood Hill Park at 218th Street and Indian Road. The rock lies west of the soccer field.

Long Before *American Idol*, There Was Amateur Night at the Apollo

On November 21, 1934—the same year that Harlem's Apollo Theater became the first upscale music hall where black performers could play for black audiences—a nervous teenage girl climbed onstage. It was Amateur Night—when wannabe stars could test their talents on a crowd that often hissed them off the stage.

The girl had planned to dance, but the seasoned Edwards Sisters had just danced up a storm. So she started singing, and the house went wild.

That was Ella Fitzgerald—the first in a spectacularly long list of musical sensations who got their start by winning Amateur Night. Sarah Vaughan won Amateur Night in 1943, James Brown in 1956, the Jackson Five in 1969. The Apollo launched the careers of dozens of other luminaries, including Billie Holiday, Jackie Wilson, Ben E. King, the Isley Brothers, Stevie Wonder, Luther Vandross, Fat Joe, Dru Hill, Lauryn Hill, and Blu Cantrel.

Visit the Apollo Theater at 253 West 125th Street, or online at www.apollotheater.org. Amateur Night still takes place every Wednesday night at 7:30.

4

Uptown East Manhattan
(North of Fifty-ninth Street, East of Fifth Avenue)

This chapter doesn't *cover nearly as much territory as the last, but Uptown East is rich—both literally and figuratively. The Upper East Side, from roughly East Fifty-Ninth to East Ninety-Sixth Street, is one of the nation's most popular retirement destinations—for multimillionaires, with the wealth most heavily concentrated along Park Avenue.*

North of Ninety-Sixth Street to the Harlem River and from the East River to Fifth Avenue lies Spanish Harlem, also known as El Barrio and East Harlem. Since the 1950s, this neighborhood has been predominantly Puerto Rican and Nuyorican—a cross between "New York" and "Puerto Rican" that mainly refers to people whose parents and grandparents emigrated from Puerto Rico.

Museum Mile—a stretch of Fifth Avenue from Eighty-Second to 110th Street—houses some of NYC's major museums: the Metropolitan Museum of Art, the Goethe-Institut New York/German Cultural Center, Neue Galerie New York, the Solomon R. Guggenheim Museum, the National Academy Museum, Cooper-Hewitt National Design Museum, the Jewish Museum, International Center of Photography, Museum of the City of New York, El Museo del Barrio, and the Museum of African Art (www.africanart.org), which just moved from Long Island City in Queens to its new location on the corner of Fifth Avenue and 110th Street.

★ ★

In this alternative NYC guidebook, I've blithely overlooked almost every institution on Museum Mile, except for some truly bizarre bits of NYC history involving the Guggenheim's controversial construction and Jacob Riis's unprecedented use of flash photography.

Central Park is west of Fifth Avenue—thus, technically on the West Side. But since some sites are much easier to access from the East Side, I've included them in Uptown East.

★ ★

Find the Bolt

Central Park

On the first springlike Saturday in early March, two European tourists watched curiously as I snapped a dozen photos of what looked like a three-inch-tall rusty nail sticking out of some rocks in Central Park. I'd reached the end of an urban treasure hunt. The "treasure" was a rusted iron bolt that was hammered into the Manhattan schist two centuries ago.

In 1811, when the city was confined to Manhattan's southern tip, Mayor DeWitt Clinton proposed a plan to develop the island north of Houston according to a grid with streets running parallel and perpendicular to each other, like the lines on a graph. Following this plan, surveyors marked the future site of each intersection by driving an iron bolt into the ground. As the city gradually expanded northward, workers laid out the streets and dislodged the bolts.

Recently, a geographer named Reuben Rose-Redwood speculated that some bolts might be left in Central Park, which wasn't conceived until 1853. The surveyors, following the 1811 plan, would have marked out intersections for all the streets between Fifty-Ninth and 110th. Since these streets were never laid out, perhaps the bolts were still there. So Rose-Redwood combed Central Park with a GPS, searching for any remaining markers. Though he scoured all the locations where the bolts should be, he found only one—near what would have been the intersection of Sixty-Fifth Street and Sixth Avenue.

After a half-hour of hunting, I located the same bolt on some large rocks just north of Sixty-Fifth Street Transverse Road. The rocks lie between two pedestrian bridges and overlook the eastern edge of the Dairy Visitor Center and Gift Shop, which is south of the same Transverse Road. The bolt is shorter than my pinky finger and hidden in plain sight—the kind of thing you'd usually "find" accidentally—by snagging your pants on it.

Since the bolt is easy to miss, plan to visit some other Central Park attractions while you're in the neighborhood. Stop by the Dairy to

The bolt is near the bottom of this photo and slightly right of center. The background includes the Dairy and the fence overlooking the Sixty-Fifth Street Transverse.

★ ★

pick up a map of major Central Park landmarks with phone numbers to call from your cell for an audio tour.

The Dairy is open daily from 10:00 a.m. to 5:00 p.m., and the money you spend at the gift shop benefits the Central Park Conservancy.

A Vicious Wit, Born and Bred in NYC

Theodore Roosevelt's oldest child, Alice Roosevelt Longworth, famously said, "The secret of eternal youth is arrested development." As First Daughter, she smoked cigarettes on the White House roof, wore a pet boa constrictor looped around her neck, ran up gambling debts, and shot at telephone poles from a train. She married Congressman Nicholas Longworth of Ohio, but had her only child with Senator William Borah of Idaho. Her father quipped famously, "I can be president of the United States, or I can attend to Alice. I cannot possibly do both!" In 1909, when William Howard Taft succeeded Theodore Roosevelt as president, Alice buried a voodoo doll of Taft's wife, Nellie, on the White House lawn.

Alice had a pillow embroidered with her motto, "If you can't say something good about someone, sit right here by me." She detested "sincere people," including her first cousin Eleanor Roosevelt, and her fifth cousin, Franklin Delano. Perhaps only the good die young; Alice survived to age ninety-six. A self-described "ambulatory Washington monument," she settled in Dupont Circle, where she consorted with the Kennedys and Nixons and delivered skewering one-liners for nearly seven decades.

Please Touch the Art

"Hoping to boost attendance and broaden its base of supporters, the Metropolitan Museum of Art launched a new initiative this week that allows patrons, for the first time ever, to prod and scratch at the classic paintings in its revered collection," reported *The Onion*, an NYC–based satirical rag, on October 5, 2009. Visitors were also encouraged

Kids love to climb on the Alice in Wonderland statue at East Seventy-Fourth Street, north of Conservatory Water in Central Park.

★ ★

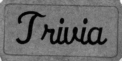

> It is illegal in New York State to greet someone by "putting one's thumb to the nose and wiggling the fingers."

to climb inside Egyptian sarcophagi and try out medieval armor and weapons.

Luckily—or unluckily, depending on your perspective—the story was fictional. Nonetheless, NYC offers an abundance of touchable public art, partly thanks to the City Beautiful Movement of the 1890s and early 1900s. This Progressive Era reform movement touted the use of fine art and architecture as a means of social control—to reduce crime, placate disgruntled factory workers, and calm middle-class anxieties about urbanization and millions of immigrants flooding the city.

Today, no one expects a stunning Guastavino vault to stop a thief from snatching your iPod, but the streets and subway stations of NYC still offer eye-catching, provocative, and *touchable* art.

A Statue You Don't Want to Meet in a Dark Alley

When it comes to public sculpture, I tend to prefer unconventional installations that create a communal experience to the more tradi-tional realistic statues of famous people. But the statue of King Jagi-ello—swords crossed over his head—stopped me in my tracks.

King Wladyslaw Jagiello united Lithuania and Poland in the 1410 Battle of Grunwald. The sculpture itself has an intriguing history. Stanislaw K. Ostrowski (1879–1947) made this bronze equestrian monument for the 1939 World's Fair in Queen's Flushing Meadows Corona Park. It stood at the entrance to the Polish Pavilion. At the end of the World's Fair, the statue was supposed to return to Poland

Fortunately, you won't meet King Jagiello in a dark alley. He's quite stationary in Central Park.

along with the rest of the Polish Pavilion, but on September 1, 1939, Nazi Germany invaded Poland—igniting World War II.

Since the statue couldn't go back to Poland as planned, New York mayor Fiorello La Guardia and parks commissioner Robert Moses asked the Polish World's Fair commission to give it to NYC. In 1945, the Polish government-in-exile placed the monument in its permanent home in Central Park.

Find King Jagiello north of Seventy-Ninth Street Transverse Road, west of East Drive, and east of Turtle Pond.

Cleopatra Did Not Knit With This Obelisk

Cleopatra's Needle has little to do with Cleopatra. It's one of two 244-ton, red granite obelisks that Thutmosis III erected in Heliopolis (near Cairo) around 1450 BCE.

The ancient Romans were wild about Egyptian obelisks and swiped as many as they could. (Today, there are thirteen Egyptian obelisks in Rome and only seven remaining in Egypt.) In 12 BCE, the emperor Augustus moved the two obelisks from Heliopolis to a temple that Cleopatra built in Alexandria—hence the name Cleopatra's Needle.

In the nineteenth century, it became fashionable to procure ancient Egyptian treasures for one's own country. In 1819, a British earl convinced an Egyptian pasha to let England have an obelisk. Thus, the first of the two "needles" at Cleopatra's temple went to London— though it took the British fifty years to get around to moving it. In 1869, the khedive of Egypt, Ismail Pasha, thought it might be nice to give the second Cleopatra's Needle to the United States as a friendly gesture to stimulate trade. At least that's the official story.

By the time Ismail's son offered the obelisk to the United States, the Egyptian people were sick of their ruler handing out national treasures. A U.S. naval officer, Lt. Comdr. Henry Honeychurch Gorringe, was charged with transporting the obelisk, but when he came for his prize, the residents of Alexandria had planned to build an apartment complex around it and had no intention of giving it up. The Egyptians

Single White Obelisk, age 3,450, height 71 feet, weight 244 tons, seeks ride back to Egypt. Let's connect.

★ ★

blocked Gorringe from moving the 71-foot, 244-ton slab of granite a mile across land to his waiting ship, so he had to transport it ten miles by water. Once he finally loaded the monument onto his ship, no Egyptian crew would sail it to the States. He had to import a Serbian crew with no seafaring experience.

The Herculean task of sailing the obelisk across the ocean and up the Hudson then lugging it across town by block and tackle took more than a year. Gorringe's pal, railroad magnate William H. Vanderbilt, financed the move with $102,567.

The obelisk would have been better off staying in Egypt, where it survived unscathed in the dry desert air for nearly thirty-five centuries. In NYC, pollution and acid rain have eroded most of the hieroglyphics in 130 years.

The obelisk towers above Central Park's Greywacke Knoll, East Side Drive at Eighty-First Street.

An Upside-Down *What*?

The Solomon R. Guggenheim Museum

The Guggenheim, one of NYC's best-loved museums, has triggered controversy and catty remarks since its inception. NYC's master builder Robert Moses dubbed the design "an upside-down cup and saucer with a silo thrown in for good luck." Moses generally preferred highways and bridges to people and art. But the Guggenheim's world-renowned architect, Frank Lloyd Wright, might not have cared much for art either.

In 1926, mining tycoon Solomon R. Guggenheim met Baroness Hilla Rebay—an abstract painter who introduced him to the works of Kandinsky, Klee, Chagall, Léger, and Mondrian. In 1937, Guggenheim created a foundation to fund abstract artists fleeing fascist dictatorships. Rebay, the first curator of the new Guggenheim Foundation, rented a space for the first Museum of Non-Objective Art, hung paintings near the floor so visitors had to sit to view them, and covered the walls in plush carpeting.

Tender Buttons

If you view the button as a mere fastener to keep your clothes from falling off, Tender Buttons will cure you of such notions. Named after a book by Gertrude Stein, this little shop sells only buttons. The interior looks like an old library card catalog room. Cabinets lining the walls brim with millions upon billions of buttons, including one of the largest-known selections of men's blazer buttons and an exquisite array of gourmet fasteners—from eighteenth-century French illustrated *boutons* to the buttons made for George Washington's inauguration, which fetch up to $17,000 at auction. Talk about a niche market.

Visit Tender Buttons at 143 East Sixty-Second Street Monday through Friday from 10:30 a.m. to 6:00 p.m., Saturday from 10:30 a.m. to 5:30 p.m., or on the web at www.tender buttons-nyc.com.

Tender Buttons. The button does so much more than hold our pants up.

★ ★

Since Guggenheim had more than enough cash to build his own museum, Rebay commissioned Wright to design a "museum temple." Wright admired the ancient Mesopotamian ziggurat—a pyramid-shaped stack of platforms with each tier smaller than the previous. Since ziggurats often harbored a king's tomb, Wright figured they symbolized death. He flipped the ziggurat on its head to symbolize life, and—since Wright hated right angles—he designed a huge beige spiral, widening from bottom to top.

The Guggenheim's interior is a cylindrical rotunda with a hollow center and a spiral ramp ascending along the walls toward a skylight. The ramp leading to the skylight might have been Rebay's influence.

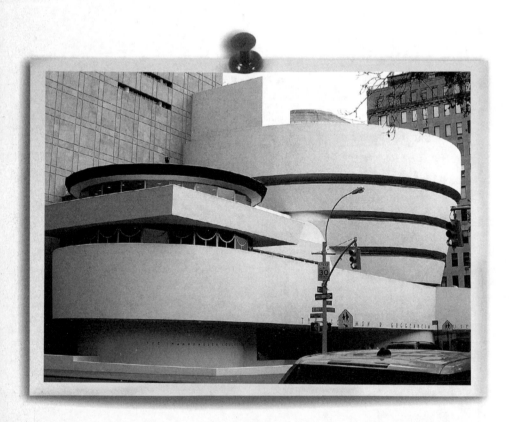

The Guggenheim. Did you know it's upside-down?

In NYC, a puppet show in your window can land you in jail for thirty days.

She believed that nonobjective art was the path to enlightenment and spiritual transcendence.

After Guggenheim's death, the board and Wright turned against Rebay. Not everyone appreciated Wright's work either. During the planning, twenty-two artists signed a letter of protest. Critics have argued that the building's design overpowers the art on display, and the rotunda's concave walls and spiral ramp don't suit the museum's function: It's hard to hang paintings on curved walls, and sculptures stand lopsided on the tilted floor.

In fact, Wright didn't seem to care that the building's purpose was to exhibit art.

When someone suggested that the walls might not be large enough to display paintings, Wright snapped that they could cut the paintings in half.

The Guggenheim, located at 1071 Fifth Avenue, is open Sunday through Wednesday from 10:00 a.m. to 5:45 p.m., Friday from 10:00 a.m. to 5:45 p.m., and Saturday from 10:00 a.m. to 7:45 p.m.

Boy Mayor Falls Out of Plane
The John Purroy Mitchel monument

It's hard to miss the bright gold bust at the East Ninetieth Street entrance to Central Park, but most New Yorkers have no idea who John Purroy Mitchel was.

Mitchel was NYC's second-youngest mayor, elected at age

★ ★

thirty-four. (The youngest was thirty-one-year-old Hugh J. Grant, a Tammany Hall Democrat, who served from 1889 to 1892.)

As a young lawyer, Mitchel made a name for himself as a corruption fighter when he successfully prosecuted the borough presidents of both Manhattan and the Bronx. As mayor from 1914 to 1918, Mitchel fought both police corruption and the Tammany Hall political machine. But Tammany Hall proved too strong, and he served only one term.

When his mayoral term ended, Mitchel joined the armed forces as a pilot. Tragically, he forgot to fasten his seatbelt during a training session and fell out of his plane.

The John Purroy Mitchel monument stands as solemn reminder to fasten your seatbelt.

Mitchel fell five hundred feet and died instantly. (You might think that no one could survive such a drop, but in 1942 and 1943, Soviet pilot I. M. Chisov and U.S. Air Force Sergeant Alan Magee survived freefalls of 20,000 feet. Chisov plunged into deep snow, and Magee shattered a skylight in a French train station. Mitchel wasn't so lucky. He hit solid ground.)

When you're finished looking at Mitchel's bust, turn 135 degrees to your left. About twenty feet away is a bronze statue of a man staring at his watch. This is Jesus Ygnacio Dominguez's sculpture of the late Fred Lebow, founder of the New York City Marathon and long-time president of the New York Road Runners Club. The statue has its permanent home at Ninetieth Street, where runners enter the park to stretch and work out together. But once a year in November, the statue is moved to a spot within view of the finish line, so Lebow can stare at his watch—timing runners as they cross.

Alligators in Sewers?

Sewer alligators may be the stuff of urban legend, but sharp-toothed reptiles occasionally turn up in NYC's more hospitable environments. In June 2001, two gator wranglers from Florida captured a two-foot-long South American spectacled caiman in the Harlem Meer, a lake on Central Park's east side between 106th and 110th Streets.

★ ★

First Building Constructed as a Mosque in NYC

The first building constructed as a mosque in NYC wasn't erected until 1989. There were mosques before then, but they occupied buildings designed for other purposes.

In contrast to almost every other structure north of Houston Street, the Islamic Cultural Center is at a 29-degree angle from the Manhattan street grid. When it comes to building mosques, it's all about direction. The entrance to a mosque must be positioned so that a person setting out from the building would travel the short-est possible distance along the Earth's surface to the Great Mosque in Mecca, Saudi Arabia. If this sounds easy to figure out, that's only because we intuitively think of the Earth as a flat surface, rather than a curved one. To calculate the shortest distance between two points on a curved surface requires a branch of math called spherical trigo-nometry. This is also why your flight from the United States to Europe might take you over northern Canada or Greenland. It seems as if your plane is heading in the wrong direction, but it's not. Picture a straight line—through the solid Earth—connecting your departure city with your destination. You're flying directly over that line.

The Islamic Cultural Center of New York is located at 201 East Ninety-Sixth Street and Third Avenue and on the web at www.islamic culturalcenter-ny.org.

Is It an Angel or the End of the World?

The photographs of Jacob Riis,
Museum of the City of New York's permanent collection

Imagine it's 1888, and you're sleeping on the floor of a 10-by-10-foot room, in a Lower East Side tenement without gaslight, heat, indoor toilets, or running water. Suddenly, a gun goes off. The room fills with blinding light. People are screaming and jumping out of windows.

It's Danish-born police reporter Jacob Riis, and he isn't firing bullets, but flash powder cartridges—an early form of flash photography.

74

Riis had been homeless himself in the early 1870s. As a police reporter, he was determined to expose the misery of the tenements. In the 1880s, the Lower East Side was the most densely populated place on earth: Roughly 334,000 immigrants and migrants lived within a single square mile, and middle-class Americans knew nothing about them.

Riis's writing didn't have the impact he wanted. But in 1887, he heard of a new way to photograph dark indoor places by firing magnesium flash powder from a pistol-like device. Riis rounded up a few photographers. In his autobiography, *The Making of an American,* he describes their first efforts: "The flashlight of those days was contained in cartridges fired from a revolver. The spectacle of half a dozen strange men invading a house in the midnight hour armed with big pistols which they shot off recklessly was hardly reassuring. . . [T]enants bolted through windows and down fire escapes wherever we went." Riis soon dispensed with the pistol lamps and lit magnesium powder in a frying pan.

Riis's groundbreaking book of photographs, *How The Other Half Lives* (1890), shocked well-heeled New Yorkers who had never seen the tenements' squalor. For the first time, they viewed the destitute immigrants as human. Though Riis was steeped in the ethnic and racial prejudices of his day and didn't believe in any government intervention to help the poor, he nonetheless exposed urban poverty and is considered a pioneer of "muckraking" journalism and Progressive Era reform.

To see Riis's photographs, visit the Museum of the City of New York at 1220 Fifth Avenue and 103rd Street, or view them online at www.authentichistory.com/1865-1897/progressive/riis/index.html.

Alligators in Sewers: An Urban Legend Is Born

On a February evening in 1935, Salvatore Condulucci, a teenager living on East 123rd Street, was shoveling snow into a manhole near the Harlem River when he spotted an 8-foot-long black creature thrashing in the icy sewage.

"An alligator!"

Salvatore and friends dangled a noose into the sewer, looped it around the reptile's neck, and dragged it out of the manhole and onto the snow. They wanted to rescue the creature, but the half-strangled alligator didn't see it this way. It snapped at the boys, and they clubbed it to death with their shovels.

The story appeared in the *New York Times* on February 10, 1935. In November 2009, Condulucci, then ninety-two, confirmed the incident for the *Times*, but couldn't say whether the reports of alligator *colonies* lurking in the city sewers were fact or fiction.

Most likely, the 1935 *Times* article spawned legends. Sewer-alligator sightings abounded that year, as a series of frantic sewer inspectors returned from underground claiming they'd barely escaped the jaws of death. Teddy May, the snaggle-toothed, tobacco-chomping superintendent of sewers, dismissed these reports.

"I says to myself, them guys been drinking in there. . . . I'll go down there and prove to youse guys that there ain't no alligators in my sewers," May rasped, according to Robert Daley's purported nonfiction book, *The World Beneath the City* (1959). But as May descended into the sewer, his flashlight beam fell on a colony of 2-foot-long crocodilians, happily paddling in the sewer pipes. According to Daley, May and his inspectors exterminated the gators with rat poison and .22 caliber rifles—"a veritable sewer safari."

But how did the gators get there in the first place? In Daley's probably fictional account, the sewer inspectors speculated that pet dealers—capitalizing on the pet turtle craze—began importing baby alligators. When the little reptiles outgrew their cuteness, their owners dumped them into an open manhole.

Thomas Pynchon amended this story in his 1961 novel *V.* Children flushed their pet alligators down the toilet, "and these had grown and reproduced, had fed off rats and sewage, so that now they moved big, blind, albino, all over the sewer system. . . . Some had turned cannibal because in their neighborhood the rats had all been eaten, or had fled in terror." And so a single incident on East 123rd Street spawned an urban legend.

Harlem's Notorious Hoarders

For several generations, NYC mothers have warned their kids, "Clean up your room, or you'll end up like the Collyer brothers." Scions of one of New York's oldest families, Homer and Langley Collyer crammed their three-story brownstone at 2078 Fifth Avenue in Harlem with more than 136 tons of rubbish.

Homer, born in 1881, and Langley, 1883, both went to Columbia. After their parents died, the brothers gradually cut themselves off from the outside world. Though millionaires, they refused to pay their utility bills. Their telephone was disconnected in 1917, their gas shut off in 1928. They used kerosene to cook and light their home and, rather than having running water in their house, they carted buckets of water from a fountain four blocks away.

While Homer worked in a law office, Langley prowled the streets picking through trash and stuffing the house with reams of newspapers, cardboard boxes, empty cans, scrap metal, tree branches, broken bicycles, umbrellas, old stove pipes, and other random garbage. He packed rubbish against the windows and doors so no one could see inside and constructed a maze of interlocking tunnels through the debris and rigged homemade booby traps, so an intruder who walked into one of the trip wires would be crushed under piles of garbage, heavy furniture, and tree limbs up to twenty inches in diameter.

In his later years, Homer went blind. He became dependent on Langley, and thereafter he was only once spotted outside helping Langley drag a tree in through the front door.

Then, on the morning of March 21, 1947, the NYPD received an anonymous call claiming that someone had died at 2078 Fifth Avenue. It took the police two hours to get inside the building. Neighbors claimed Langley went in and out through a hole in the basement, but the police couldn't find an entrance: All the doors and windows were barricaded with trash.

When an officer finally managed to enter with a ladder through an upper-story window, he found the emaciated body of Homer Collyer.

For two weeks, the police combed the house and the city for Langley. They removed more than one hundred tons of trash from the building. The project was deadly: In every room and hallway, booby traps threatened to crush investigators under piles of rubbish.

Finally, on April 8—eighteen days after discovering Homer's body—detectives found Langley less than ten feet from where his brother had lain. He had apparently been crawling through one of the two-foot-wide tunnels in the maze he'd built, when he accidentally set off one of his own booby traps.

The brownstone was torn down later that year. Collyer Brothers Park now occupies the site on Fifth Avenue at East 128th Street. With the help of GreenThumb community gardening program, neighborhood groups planted a lush garden. For all the ghost stories in NYC, one doesn't hear of Langley or Homer haunting the site. There's simply not enough trash around.

CHAPTER

5

Brooklyn

The Dutch called it Breuckelen or "Broken Land," but no one seems to think it needs to be fixed—at least not geographically. I'm quite partial to Brooklyn, and I'm not alone. With 2.6 million residents, Brooklyn is NYC's most populous borough and the second most densely populated county in the United States, after Manhattan. If Brooklyn seceded from NYC, it would be the nation's fourth-largest metropolis.

Coney Island is Brooklyn's undisputed capital of quirk. Before movies and TV, Coney Island amusement parks wowed thrill-seekers with disaster reenactments of Mount Pelée's 1902 volcanic eruption, the 1906 San Francisco earthquake, the fall of ancient Pompeii, and the Boer War, starring real-life Boer general Piet Cronje and one thousand soldiers firing blanks at each other. A reenactment of the 1900 Galveston Flood involved both real and so-called fake water. (I don't know what "fake water" is, but I'm picturing blue cardboard cut in the shape of waves.)

The fires, on the other hand, weren't always fake. In "Fighting the Flames"—a favorite show at the Dreamland amusement park—a six-story, iron hotel was actually set ablaze. Two thousand fire fighters saved real people trapped inside.

Some nondisasters were popular, too. In "A Trip to the Moon," sixty passengers boarded a spaceship, looked out over the (painted canvas) scenery through portholes, then deplaned in a moon crater, where dwarves dressed as "Selenites" with spiked backs welcomed them.

★ ★

You'll read plenty about Coney Island in the following pages. Having resided in several Brooklyn neighborhoods—Prospect Heights, Clinton Hill, Crown Heights, and Park Slope—I'd like to plug a few of the borough's main attractions that didn't make it into the chapter. I once had the great fortune of living across the street from the nation's second-largest public art museum—the Brooklyn Museum (vvvvw.brooklynmuseum.org) at 200 Eastern Parkway. Go there. You'd hear much more about it, if it didn't have such stiff competition across the river. After the Brooklyn Museum, check out the neighboring Brooklyn Botanical Gardens (www.bbg.org) and Prospect Park (www.prospectpark.org). Frederick Law Olmsted and Calvert Vaux, who also designed Central Park, considered Prospect Park their masterpiece.

While you're in Crown Heights, a short drive or subway ride will take you to three historic houses that belonged to a mid-nineteenth-century community of free blacks. The Weeksville Heritage Center at 1698 Bergen Street (www.weeksvillesociety.org) celebrates the thriving African-American community that James Weeks founded in 1838.

"If You Believe That, I've Got a Bridge to Sell You"

The idea of selling the Brooklyn Bridge has long been a joke and an example of the consummate scam. In fact, con artists began peddling the bridge as soon as it was completed in 1883. In the 1880s and 1890s, swindler Reed C. Waddell waited until the cops were out of sight, then posted signs advertising, Bridge for Sale.

Turn-of-the-century conman George C. Parker, who also trafficked in the Statue of Liberty, the Metropolitan Museum of Art, and Grant's Tomb, forged documents proving that he owned the bridge and persuaded buyers they could make a chunk of change by charging a toll. The cops had to remove some trusting customers who were building tollgates on their new purchase.

Alas, nobody's buying the Brooklyn Bridge these days.

81

★ ★

Trivia

While watching TV in their Brooklyn home, two brothers found a four-foot boa constrictor between the couch cushions.

Bridge peddlers preyed on immigrants fresh off the boat. In the late 1800s, the Brooklyn Bridge was an easy sell. Its size made it easy to advertise. Immigrants couldn't miss it as they came into port. By the 1920s, authorities at Ellis Island were passing out leaflets that read, "You can't buy public buildings or streets."

One of the best ways to see the Brooklyn Bridge is to walk or bike across the wide, elevated pedestrian walkway. In Brooklyn, pedestrians can access the walkway near the auto entrance at Tillary and Adams Streets or via a staircase on Prospect Street between Cadman Plaza East and West. In Manhattan, pedestrians can enter the walkway from the end of Centre Street or via the free-access south staircase of the Brooklyn Bridge/City Hall subway station.

Famous Nineteenth-Century Sex Scandal
Plymouth Church of the Pilgrims

There's a lot to see at Plymouth Church of the Pilgrims. Along with a chunk of Plymouth Rock, the actual granodiorite upon which the Mayflower landed, your tour guide will show you the tunnel-like cellar under the church sanctuary, where runaway slaves hid on their way to Canada.

The church's first and most celebrated preacher, Henry Ward Beecher, made Plymouth Church into "the Grand Central Depot" of the Underground Railroad, a secret network of civilians who helped slaves escape to freedom. At a time when clerics were run out of town for preaching abolition, Beecher spouted his beliefs with fervor—literally stomping on the chains that had bound John Brown and staging mock "slave auctions," in which he urged his congregation

Outside Plymouth Church stands a statue of Henry Ward Beecher—abolitionist preacher, nineteenth-century Elvis.

to purchase slaves from their masters. At Sunday service on February 5, 1860, the congregation filled the collection plates with $900 and a gold ring to free a young slave girl named Pinky. Placing the ring on Pinky's finger, Beecher proclaimed, "With this ring, I thee wed—to freedom!" (On Plymouth's eightieth anniversary in 1927, Pinky gave the ring back to the church, where it's still displayed.)

Beecher's dramatic flair drew an illustrious following. He hobnobbed with Susan B. Anthony, Elizabeth Cady Stanton, Walt Whitman, and Mark Twain. Even Abraham Lincoln numbered among his fans.

Women swooned over Beecher—not only because he championed their right to vote. His extramarital frolics included Elizabeth Tilton, the wife of close friend and colleague Theodore Tilton. Beecher and Theodore wanted to cover up the affair, but the secret leaked out when Theodore told Elizabeth Cady Stanton, who in turn told Victoria Woodhull, a fellow suffragist, radical free love advocate, and the first woman to run for president.

Angry that Beecher wouldn't support her presidential candidacy, Woodhull publicized his philanderings in an issue of her newspaper. The women definitely got the short end of the stick. Woodhull was jailed for sending obscene materials through the mail. Plymouth Church held an inquiry and found Beecher innocent, but excommunicated Elizabeth Tilton. (In the 1870s, the mere soupçon of well-heeled ladies having any sex—let alone extramarital sex—triggered mass fainting spells.)

Theodore then sued Beecher for "criminal conversation"—Victorian legalese for "adultery." The "Trial of the Century" lasted from January to July 1875. No one except Beecher's wife Eunice doubted the affair, but Beecher's oratory bewitched the jurors, and they could not reach a verdict.

Though Beecher wasn't convicted, his reputation never fully recovered. Even today, Plymouth Church devotes a page of their website to Beecher, but carefully sidesteps the sex scandal.

Visit the church at 75 Hicks Street, or online at www.plymouth church.org.

Accidental Revolutionary
War Re-Enactment

In 2007, Duke Riley, an artist fascinated with wild urban waterfronts, built a replica of the first submarine ever used in battle. The *Turtle*, invented in 1775, was rudimentary by today's submarine standards. A single operator maneuvered the egg-shaped vessel with hand-cranked propellers, drilled into the hull of a British ship, and implanted a keg of gunpowder.

In September 1776, as the British prepared to attack New York, the Patriots sent the *Turtle* to attach a mine to a British ship moored off of Governor's Island. The plan failed, and the *Turtle* never again saw combat.

Or maybe it did.

Riley and two cohorts claimed they hadn't meant to attack a British ship in August 2007, when they launched their handmade *Turtle* from Red Hook, Brooklyn. But the RMS *Queen Mary 2* just happened to be docked in Red Hook's Brooklyn Cruise Terminal.

The coast guard spotted an unidentified sinking object, towed by an inflatable boat, within two hundred feet of the luxury liner's bow. Riley was cited for operating an unsafe vessel and for breaching a security zone.

Parrots and Pyramids
Green-Wood Cemetery

When you don't want to brave the crowds in Central or Prospect Park, Green-Wood Cemetery is quiet and peaceful even on a sun-drenched weekend. You can't play Frisbee (without hitting the tomb-stones), but you'll lose yourself on the winding paths, stumble upon breathtaking views of the New York Harbor, and walk for hours with-out anyone in sight. Just make sure to bring a watch or cell phone. The guards lock the gates at five o'clock sharp, and they don't check to make sure everyone's out. If you lose track of time, you might end up at a sleepover with those whose slumber never ends.

Among the six hundred thousand graves, you'll find the markers of Jean-Michel Basquiat (1960–1988), Henry Ward Beecher (1813–1887),

Glaciers Dumped Brooklyn and Queens off the Coast

Fifty thousand years ago, at the peak of the last ice age, northern North America lay under a thousand feet of ice that reached as far south as Staten Island. The tremendous weight of the ice crushed the rock underneath, and the glaciers acted like giant conveyor belts—stripping the top layers of rock and sediment and dumping them off the northeast coast. Brooklyn and Queens are composed of piles of sediment that the glaciers picked up and dropped into the ocean. This vast glacier dump created the archipelago that includes Cape Cod, Nan-tucket, Martha's Vineyard, as well as Long Island.

Van Ness Parsons Pyramid in Green-Wood Cemetery. I never knew the Virgin Mary and the Sphinx were friends.

Leonard Bernstein (1918–1990), Margaret Sanger (1879–1966), and William Marcy "Boss" Tweed (1823–1878).

One of the most bizarre monuments, the Van Ness Parsons Pyramid, stands at the intersection of Bayview and Battle Avenues, not far from the main gate. Built for amateur Egyptologist Albert Ross Parsons (1847–1933) and his family, the pyramid features statues of Madonna and Child, Zodiac symbols, and the Sphinx—that Egyptian woman-headed lion who doesn't usually hang out with Jesus Christ.

Be sure to look for green feathers in the Gothic spire of the main gate. A flock of wild Quaker parrots—endemic to the subtropical and temperate Argentina—have made the spire their home. Feral colonies live as far north as Connecticut and Rhode Island, but no one knows how the parrots got to Brooklyn. Some claim that, during the 1960s, thieves plundered a shipment that arrived at the airport. But when they opened the crate, parrots flew out. Steve Baldwin maintains the premier website on Brooklyn's parrots (www.brooklynparrots.com) and leads Wild Brooklyn Parrot Safaris several times a year.

Green-Wood Cemetery's main entrance at 500 Twenty-Fifth Street is open daily, weather permitting, from 8:00 a.m. to 5:00 p.m. Hours are extended from 7:00 a.m. to 7:00 p.m. from Memorial Day weekend until Labor Day. Go to www.green-wood.com for more details.

Brooklyn Superhero Supply Company

Like any self-respecting superhero, you know the importance of buying supplies from a reputable source. A single snag in your invisibility cloak could betray you to your nemesis.

Flying over the five boroughs, you've no doubt trained your telescopic vision on the Park Slope storefront: "Brooklyn's #1 Source for Telekinesis." (Thank God! The stuff you picked up at that warehouse in Sydney won't even bend spoons!) You've also noted the "Wide Selection of Subatomic Sizes" for your particle gun, as well as the company's concern for superhero safety: "Exposed to Radiation Experiments? Check Our Mutation Charts for What to Expect." You

**Brooklyn Superhero Supply Company may be the
only place in town that sells gravity by the gallon
and a forty-six ounce Apprehended Blob.**

land on the sidewalk and politely check your X-ray glasses at the front desk. Holy laser beam, Batman! This store has everything.

- Forcefield Generators
- Wonder Woman–style Deflector Bracelets
- Mylar Force Fields
- Antigravity, sold by the gallon
- Mutant Mind Probes
- Evil Blob Containment Capsules
- Antimatter
- Bugayenko brand thirty-two-ounce and half-gallon bottles of Invisibility, Shape-shifting, Time Travel, Elasticity, ESP, Sonar, Chaos, and Cloning Fluid

★ ★

- Robotic Sharks to guard your underwater lair
- Run-Arrest, a fast-drying formula for halting runs in leotards, tights, capes, gloves, hoods (probably works on pantyhose too)
- Sidekick Placement Services
- Superhero's Map of Brooklyn, with well-marked landing pads, side-kick training grounds, ripples in space-time, and more
- Mind Reader: "The best criminal interrogation tool known to man. Also makes a wonderful boyfriend."
- And last but not least—"Strive To Be Boring" Secret Identity Kits.

So who shops at the Superhero Supply Company? Captain America? The Incredible Hulk?

As it turns out, the Superhero Supply Company is itself a secret identity. Once you get past the storefront, you'll find 826NYC, a non-profit that writer Dave Eggers founded to help kids with creative and expository writing skills. (Note the clever inversion of Superman taking on the secret identity of writer Clark Kent.)

So the next time you soar over Brooklyn faster than the speed of sound, come in for a landing at Brooklyn Superhero Supply Company, 372 Fifth Avenue, or buy your force fields online at www.superhero supplies.com. All proceeds from the sale of Antimatter and other goods go to support 826NYC's free writing and tutoring programs. And if your nemesis comes looking for you in the store, you can always disguise yourself as a writing tutor.

"They came. They ate. They conquered. All in 12 minutes."
Hot Dog Eating Wall of Fame

Nathan's Famous Fourth of July International Hot Dog Eating contest doesn't only involve chocking down double-digit pounds of tube steak. The "gurgitators" (as opposed to "regurgitators") must hold it down until the contest officially ends. An unintended hork disqualifies even the best-trained tummy.

According to Nathan's, the first contest took place in 1916, the same year that Polish immigrants Nathan and Ida Handwerker opened

The countdown clock shows 85 days, 40 minutes,
and 2.7 seconds until the next gorge.
BOBBY MORGAN

their nickel hot dog stand in Coney Island. Today, on the Stillwell
Avenue side of Nathan's, a towering Wall of Fame lists each year's
winner since 1988, regaled by the motto, "They came. They ate. They
conquered. All in 12 minutes." A digital countdown clock displays the
days, hours, minutes, and seconds until the next binge-a-thon.

In 2001, Takeru Kobayashi took the contest to a new level by gob-
bling 50 franks in 12 minutes—doubling the prior record of 25. A
year later, he set the world's cow-brain-eating record by inhaling 17.7
pounds of bovine mental matter in 15 minutes.

But Takeru no longer holds the hot dog gold: In 2007, Joey Chest-
nut devoured Takeru's record by swallowing 66, then consumed his
own record in 2009 with 68. Takeru was almost disqualified in the

final seconds of the 2007 contest for a "Roman method incident" (aka "reversal of fortune").

One contest regular, NYC's own Jason "Crazy Legs" Conti, starred in the 2004 documentary *Crazy Legs Conti: Zen and the Art of Competitive Eating*: "Eccentric New York window washer, nude model, and sperm donor, Crazy Legs Conti uses Zen techniques as he strives to become a professional eater." Joey, Takeru, and Crazy Legs all have websites, Facebook pages, Twitter accounts, fans, and groupies.

As for Nathan's, any place open ninety-five years has stories. One summer, Nathan Handwerker went out of town and left his son Murray in charge of the restaurant. A man who had just caught a whale approached Murray and offered to leave the largest of mammals in front of Nathan's to attract customers. For several days, a crowd thronged around the dead leviathan. The restaurant set record sales until a heat wave struck. When Nathan returned, he smelled the rotting corpse from a mile away and found no customers in sight. All publicity is not good publicity.

Find Nathan's Famous at 1310 Surf Avenue in Coney Island and online at www.nathansfamous.com.

Trivia

In 2007, a Brooklyn resident found a seven-foot python curled inside her toilet. The snake had wriggled up the pipes to her third-story apartment.

Step Right Up and See the Premature Babies

From 1903 to 1944, Coney Island's Luna Park featured attractions like A Trip to the Moon, Hagenbeck's Wild Animals, and the ever-popular Infant Incubators—live premature babies on display alongside Sword Swallowers and Bearded Ladies.

You may find the idea of preemies as a freak-show exhibit rather horrifying, but in the early 1900s, premature babies had lower

"Infant Incubators with Live Infants" in Luna Park, circa 1905.
DETROIT PUBLISHING COMPANY PHOTOGRAPH COLLECTION, LIBRARY OF CONGRESS

★ ★

Shaking a dust mop out a window is a crime in NYC.

mortality rates and received better care in a Coney Island amusement park than in any hospital in the United States.

Most hospitals didn't adopt special care baby units until after World War II. When Parisian doctor Martin A. Couney brought incubators to the United States in 1903, NYC hospitals rejected the new technology. Intent on saving the preemies, Dr. Couney took his incubators to Coney Island. Luna Park was thrilled to display puppy-size humans—most under three pounds—lined up under heaters and breathing filtered air. Though the medical establishment shunned Dr. Couney as a crass showman, the exhibit was medically sound. Nurses cared for the babies in a sterile environment with hospital-like conditions. According to contemporary news reports, all the babies survived. At a time when premature babies rarely made it, Dr. Couney saved 6,500 lives.

Couney died in 1950, but in June 2005, some infant veterans of the exhibit came to see their doctor inducted into the Coney Island Hall of Fame. Twins George and Norma Johnson weighed less than 4.5 pounds together when they were born on July 3, 1937. Their father was poor, and Dr. Couney offered to put the newborns in the incubator for free, as long as the Johnsons didn't mind having their twins displayed on Coney Island.

The Coney Island Amateur Psychoanalytic Society

Several years ago, media artist Zoe Beloff was watching some old home movies she'd bought at the Chelsea Flea Market. She'd long been fascinated by how home movies betray people's unconscious desires and fears, but these films were uncommonly overt. In "The Bear Dream" (1937), for instance, a man turns into a tame bear and enjoys the food and affection women lavish on him."

Research led Beloff to the Coney Island Amateur Psychoanalytic

Model of Albert Grass's proposed Dreamland amusement park.
BRAD PARIS, COURTESY OF ZOE BELOFF

★ ★

Society. In the 1920s, Albert Grass rallied a group of Freudian enthusiasts—mostly working-class Jews and Italians—who met in a Surf Avenue office to psychoanalyze themselves and make movies. Not long after Kodak introduced the handheld Cine-Kodak camera and sixteen-millimeter acetate safety film in 1923, the society began making home movies for self-analysis.

In his notebooks, Grass designed a new Dreamland. But while the original Dreamland was meant to amuse, Grass wanted to rebuild an amusement park with a nobler purpose—to interpret dreams based on the theories of Sigmund Freud.

Grass's Dreamland included funhouse mirrors labeled "Ego," "Superego," and "Id"; the "Psychic Censor," a baby doll rotating slowly on top of a tower; and a ride dubbed "Engines of the Id and the Psychical Apparatus" with bumper cars marked "Hysterical Phobia," "Infantile Impulse," and "Sadistic Symptom." Freud would never have approved of this unorthodox spin on psychoanalysis, but Grass certainly wasn't the last to marry Freud and pop culture.

Unfortunately, Edward Tilyou, Steeplechase amusement park's proprietor, replied to Grass's proposal: "I do not Believe [*sic*] that the public would enjoy your medical attractions which appear to cater to rather prurient tastes."

Grass's notebooks yellowed for nearly seventy years—until Beloff found them and constructed a model of Dreamland based on his sketches.

Those who missed Beloff's exhibit, "Dreamland: The Coney Island Amateur Psychoanalytic Society and Its Circle, 1926–1972," at the Coney Island Museum can still watch the remarkable home movies at www.zoebeloff.com/pages/dream_films.html.

Carnies and Rubes

Coney Island Museum and Sideshows By the Seashore

Your host, Donny Vomit, juggles chainsaws and hammers nails through his nostrils and into his skull. Princess Ananka from Cairo hypnotizes an albino Burmese python, while her husband, Ravi the Bendable Boy from Bombay, ties himself in knots. "The World's Most Partially Illustrated Woman," Insectavora Angelica allegedly lived on insects while orphaned on Fiji and performs an act called "X-Rated Fire from Below." See them all at Sideshows by the Seashore, the last surviving ten-in-one circus sideshow.

Dick D. Zigun, who founded and produces Sideshows by the Seashore, earned an MFA at Yale School of Drama and has devoted much of his life to preserving Coney Island, American popular theater, and "honky-tonk" carnival culture. In 1980, he co-founded the non-profit arts group Coney Island USA and also produces the Mermaid Parade. Each year on the Saturday closest to Summer Solstice, the Mermaid Parade draws thousands of wildly dressed sea creatures, trident-armed Poseidons, and, of course, mermaids.

Sideshows by the Seashore and the Coney Island Museum share a building from 1917 that housed Dave Rosen's Wonderland Circus Sideshow in the 1950s and 1960s. The museum features Ric Burns's fascinating and disturbing documentary *Coney Island* and a few rooms of randomly displayed and largely unexplained sideshow memorabilia:

- Pickled polydactyl hands and feet
- Disembodied teeth
- Photographs of Sealo the Seal Boy and a three-legged girl
- Two-headed deer mount with stitches suspiciously holding the necks together
- Skeleton of "The Infamous One-Armed Squirrel of Prospect Park"
- Stuffed, two-faced rodent standing upright on four hind legs
- Mutoscope that charges a penny for a hand-cranked, flip-card movie of Thomas Edison electrocuting poor Topsy the Elephant—a true low point in human-pachyderm relations. (The *Coney Island*

★ ★

"The Infamous One-Armed Squirrel of Prospect Park."
Doubters say the carnies pulled an arm off a four-
legged skeleton, but I believe.

film also contains a clip of Topsy's death, which haunted me for days afterward. Parents Strongly Cautioned: If I'd seen this at ten, I wouldn't have slept for weeks.)

The museum was well worth the $1 admission fee. One of my companions told the girl at the counter that he'd had a relationship with "Impervious Aziza," who tread on broken glass, ate light bulbs, and lay on a bed of nails while people broke concrete blocks on her chest. Later we learned that the admissions fee was actually 99 cents. We'd each been "taken" for a penny, but we didn't mind. We were, after all, the rubes in this equation.

The Coney Island Museum at 1208 Surf Avenue is open year-round on Saturdays and Sundays from noon to 5:00 p.m. Check out www.coneyisland.com/museum.shtml.

★ ★

Also at 1208 Surf Avenue, Sideshows by the Seashore takes place during the summer on Tuesdays and Wednesdays from 2:00 p.m. to 8:00 p.m. and on Saturdays and Sundays from 1:00 p.m. to 8:00 p.m. For the schedule and full menu of human curiosities, check out www .coney island.com/sideshow.shtml.

My Only Ride on the Cyclone
The Coney Island Cyclone

When West Virginia coal miner Emilio Franco boarded the Coney Island Cyclone in 1949, he hadn't spoken in six years. Doctors had diagnosed him with aphonia but hadn't found the cause. As the train climbed the eighty-six-foot hill of the rickety roller coaster, Franco was mute as usual, according to his cousin who sat beside him. But on the sixty-degree drop, Franco howled. Stumbling off the ride less than two minutes later, he turned to his cousin and said, "I feel sick."

While Franco may be the Cyclone's only reported miracle cure, millions of fans have raved about the Cyclone since it opened on June 26, 1927. Charles Lindbergh told *Time* magazine that a ride on the Cyclone was more exciting than his first solo flight across the Atlantic Ocean.

The Cyclone is a "woodie" with steel rails laid on a wooden track. Many riders—including me—find the creaks, groans, and possible wood rot much scarier than the hair-raising drops or 180-degree turns.

Nonetheless, a native New Yorker who'd braved the Cyclone hundreds of times, convinced me that it was a necessary rite of passage.

On a windy, overcast day, we climbed into the roller coaster car, which seemed little more than a church pew with sides. The operator lowered a single padded bar across our laps and locked it in place. That was it. No seatbelts, and lots of wiggle room. That bar would have held a 350-pound man in place quite snugly, but I weigh a third of that, and the padded bar was all that kept me from flying into the air over Luna Park.

★ ★

The Coney Island Cyclone has been known to make the mute scream.

I didn't puke on the Cyclone. But that was only because at each of those 180-degree turns and 60-degree drops my body left my stomach behind. It was like riding in a down elevator that suddenly went into freefall then veered in unpredictable directions.

Finally the car screeched to a stop, and I staggered out.

Still in the car, my friend looked slightly hurt. "You don't want to go again?"

Take a chance riding the Cyclone at 834 Surf Avenue and West Tenth Street, or if you're not feeling brave enough, check out the ride at www.coneyislandcyclone.com.

"Mother-in-Law"
Horseradish and Mustard

Does your mother-in-law make your eyes water and nose run? Apparently mothers-in-law aren't much more popular in Russia than in the United States.

On the way back from Coney Island, stop by the Russian enclave of Brighton Beach. At M&I International Foods, you can buy Mother-in-Law-brand mustard and horseradish, along with a wide range of other Slavic and Eastern European delicacies.

Located at 249 Brighton Beach Avenue, M&I International Foods is open daily from 8:00 a.m. to 10:00 p.m.

The "Mother-in-Law" brand name appears on the label in Cyrillic.

ЗАКУСОН

ЯДРЁНАЯ

ТЁЩИН ХРЕН
GOURMET HORSERADISH
NET WT. 8.8 OZ (250 g/rp)

HOT
КРЕПКАЯ

A Perfect *Schmatta*

The Yiddish word *schmatta* means "rags" and often refers to the frumpy old dresses women wear to do chores—as in "Don't you leave this house in that old *schmatta*."

In the 1940s and 1950s, many Jewish immigrants also used the word fondly to describe the textile industry in New York City.

If you need a new *schmatta*, you can purchase a tent-style Moo Moo dress at Vienti at 268 Brighton Beach Avenue.

6

Queens

Queens occupies 109 *square miles—more than one-third of NYC's total landmass. It's also the nation's most diverse county: An estimated 48.1 percent of its residents were foreign-born. The 2010 census will likely show that immigrants now make up over 50 percent of Queens' total population.*

One way to experience some of this diversity is to ride the 7 train from Forty-Second Street/Times Square to Main Street/Flushing. This subway line is known as the International Express because it passes through a number of immigrant communities and has an ethnically diverse, international ridership.

The 7 train will take you to most of the sites in this chapter, and it runs on elevated tracks in Queens, offering great views of the urban landscape. Catch the 7 in Times Square or at Grand Central. Shortly after the train bursts out of the tunnel into Queens, look for a factory complex entirely covered in graffiti. This is 5Pointz Aerosol Art Center (www.5ptz.com) at 46-23 Crane Street. The factory fills an entire block of Jackson Avenue between Crane and Davis Streets. For the best aerial view, keep your eyes peeled between the second and third station stops in Queens—Hunters Point Avenue and Forty-Fifth Road/Courthouse Square.

Stay on the 7 train until the 111th Street stop at Flushing Meadow Corona Park. Walk south on 111th Street and enter the park to visit the Queens Zoo, Queens Museum of Art, and the remaining structures from the 1964 World's Fair. These sites are spread out, so plan to walk or rent a bike near the Passarelle Building at the park's north entrance. You'll find tree-climbing deer, amorous bears, tiny buildings you can adopt on a to-scale model of NYC, and Googie-style towers that look like the Jetsons' Skypad Apartments—all described in the following pages.

A few blocks northwest of the 111th Street Station, you can also visit the Louis Armstrong House Museum at 34-56 107th Street. As the website (www.louisarmstronghouse.org) points out, the world's most renowned jazz musician could have settled anywhere, but in 1943 he and his wife, Lucille, moved to Queens. With Ella Fitzgerald and Count Basie, Armstrong made the borough a jazz epicenter.

After visiting some sites in and near Flushing Meadows Corona Park, take the 7 two stops further to its terminus at Flushing/Main Street. Flushing's Chinatown—the nation's second-largest Chinese enclave—is less crowded than Manhattan's Chinatown and offers a huge selection of Chinese, Taiwanese, and Korean food at great prices.

After you've sampled some cuisine in Flushing, check out the Ganesh Hindu Temple (www.nyganeshtemple.org) at 45-57 Bowne Street. It's not hard to find, since nothing else in the vicinity comes close to looking like a Hindu temple. Check the website for hours and special events.

Trivia

If you buy a Coke in NYC, stop right where you are. Don't leave the store, and by all means, don't walk down the street. It is a crime to transport carbonated beverages without a permit.

Moo

Queens Zoo

At the Queens Zoo, a black bull with a wide white stripe around his middle charged at me several times. Fortunately, there was a fence between us, and he stopped before bulldozing through it. I took this as a friendly overture. As it turns out, he's a belted Galloway, or "Oreo bull," and a Yankees fan. We talked a bit about their last season before I had to leave.

In addition to numerous barnyard animals, the zoo features wildlife

I made a new friend at the Queens Zoo.

★ ★

from the Americas, including three pronghorn antelope, buffalo, California sea lions, aging rock stars, zealots from at least three political parties, and one rare Alaskan ex-governor.

Owned by the Wildlife Conservation Society, the Queens Zoo is committed to protecting the world's biodiversity, so don't miss the endangered species: The pudu, the world's tiniest deer, are native to Argentina and Chile, 14-inches-tall at the shoulder, and climb trees. Another star attraction is a romantically inclined couple of Andean bears, also called spectacled bears due to beige markings around the eyes and nose on an otherwise black coat. As members of an endangered species, Spangles and Cisco were matched up in 2006 in hopes that they'd breed—online dating hadn't worked for either of them. At nineteen, Spangles is nearing the end of her fertility, but she's clearly still frisky. Don't even think about feeding her.

You can visit the Andean bears, Oreo bulls, and other zoological wonders 365 days a year at 53-51 111th Street at the west end of Flushing Meadows Corona Park, across from Grand Central Parkway, or on the web at www.queenszoo.org. The zoo is open 10:00 a.m. to 4:30 p.m. from November through March. From April through October, the hours are 10:00 a.m. to 5:00 p.m. Monday through Friday, and 10:00 a.m. to 5:30 p.m. on weekends and holidays.

As mentioned above, the zoo is committed to protecting biodiversity, so if you're single and seeking, you should definitely stop by. The staff spends so much time on mammalian match-making that they just might have your perfect other half.

Unreal Estate

Panorama of the City of New York, Queens Museum of Art (QMA)

Where in the five boroughs can you own an apartment for $50, buy a house for $250, and erect a new condo building for $10,000? In the Panorama of the City of New York, also known as the mini-city or mini-NYC.

Built to scale with one inch equaling one hundred feet, the

The Queens Museum is selling structures on the Panorama. Want to buy a bridge?

Panorama is the largest to-scale urban model ever made. The 9,335-square-foot model represents 320 square miles of the five boroughs, 771 miles of shoreline, and 895,000 structures corresponding to every single building built before 1992.

QMA closed the mini-city from 2005 to 2007 for repair and maintenance, including the replacement of tens of thousands of itty-bitty, burnt-out light bulbs. (I don't know how many architectural-model-maintenance workers it took to screw them in.)

To cover the mini-city's ongoing maintenance costs, in 2009 QMA launched the Adopt-a-Building program. If you can't afford real estate in NYC, you can now own your own "home" on the panorama. QMA will even award you a property deed.

Adopt-a-Building will alter the panorama for the first time in nearly two decades. Most structures in the mini-city have remained largely

★ ★

unchanged since workers updated 60,000 buildings in 1992. The twin towers still stand. Under Adopt-a-Building, you can adopt existing structures or build your own.

Why bother with pesky rentals or real estate agents when you can buy a $50 apartment at QMA? Located in the New York City Building (behind the Unisphere) in Flushing Meadows Corona Park, QMA is open from noon to 6:00 p.m. Wednesday through Sunday and on Fridays from noon to 8:00 p.m. in July and August. Visit them online at www.queensmuseum.org, or call (718) 592-9700.

Manhattanhenge

Thousands of years from now, archaeologists may dig up Manhattan and think it was a giant sundial. Twice yearly, the setting sun aligns with the Manhattan street grid—illuminating both north and south sides of every east-west street on the grid. To witness this event, you have to be able to see the sun set on the horizon. Go as far east as you can on a street that provides a clear view across the island to New Jersey. Some especially good vistas include Fourteenth Street, Nineteenth (at First Avenue), Thirty-Fourth, Forty-Second (on the Tudor City Bridge), and Fifty-Seventh. From Queens or Roosevelt Island, you can also gaze across the East River, down a Manhattan cross-street, and watch the sun set over New Jersey.

Neil deGrasse Tyson—the astrophysicist who named Manhattanhenge after Stonehenge—thinks this phenomenon is unique to Manhattan. Though many other cities have rectangular street grids, the streets don't offer a clear view to the horizon.

If the Manhattan grid were aligned with geographic north, Manhattanhenge would take place on the spring and autumn equinoxes. But since the grid is rotated 28.9 degrees from geographic north, the event happens around the end of May (Memorial Day) and mid-July (baseball's All-Star break). Tyson writes, "Future anthropologists might conclude that, via the Sun, the people who called themselves Americans worshipped War and Baseball." And they wouldn't be far from the truth.

Even the Art World Loves a Good Food Fight

Art and food fights don't generally mix. Art often entails meticulous arrangement and technique, while food fights are wild free-for-alls with flying globs of digestible goo.

But in August 2009, a thousand toga-clad spectators cheered, as the warriors, sporting gladiator helmets with upside-down plastic brooms as plumage, wielded baguettes and tomatoes. Brooklyn-based artist Duke Riley staged this Roman-style gladiatorial sea battle also known as a *naumachia* in the reflecting pool outside the Queens Museum of Art (QMA). The QMA–sponsored event, titled *Those About to Die Salute You*, featured seventy thousand gallons of water, four ships Riley built for the occasion, and four warring teams, drawn from the staff of QMA, the Brooklyn Museum, the Bronx Museum of Art, and Manhattan's El Museo del Barrio. Though the ships sank promptly, photos of the event are available online at www.flickr.com/photos/brooklyn_museum/sets/72157621837808043.

Ruins of the Future
New York State Pavilion

It's hard not to imagine what the future holds, but we're often wrong. In the early 1960s, a lot of people thought that by the year 2000, we'd be living on Mars. Hardly anyone thought we'd be living online.

The designers of the 1964 World's Fair built a space-age city, complete with giant mainframe computers and NASA rockets. Bell

Aviation promised individual rocket packs to carry you through the air. Disney created its signature robots, including dinosaurs and cavemen, Abraham Lincoln reciting the Gettysburg Address, and a troupe of dolls and animals that danced and sang, "It's a Small World." On General Motors' *Futurama II* ride, passengers viewed animated scenes of a trip to the moon, an underwater resort hotel, and machines paving a jungle and building an elevated superhighway. In short, *Futurama II* promised environmental destruction for the sake of human habitation and industry.

After the fair, some pavilions became permanent fixtures like the Queens Museum of Art. Other pavilions were disassembled, shipped to other cities and states, and converted into hotels, ski lodges, churches, shopping malls, and amusement parks. The Disney robots returned to California, got lucrative jobs at Disneyland, and became forerunners of a huge audio-animatronics empire. But one of the fair's architectural marvels, the New York State Pavilion, stayed in Flushing Meadows Corona Park and languished.

Before you hop on the 7 train to visit the ruins, check out what the pavilion looked like in 1964. Some of the best pictures are online at www.westland.net/ny64fair/map-docs/newyork.htm. Designed by Phillip Johnson, the New York State Pavilion featured three Astro-View observation towers: Iconic examples of mid-twentieth-century Googie architecture, the towers were real-life equivalents of the Jetsons' Skypad Apartments in Orbit City—flying saucers on top of tall poles. Elevators whisked passengers up the outside of the towers to the observation decks. Below the towers, a circle of sixteen 98-foot concrete pillars supported a suspension roof larger than a football field, called the Tent of Tomorrow. The floor displayed a giant roadmap of New York State, made of terrazzo tile.

Unfortunately, the New York State Pavilion fell into disrepair during the 1970s. The observation towers and their elevators haven't been used in forty-five years. Vandals smashed the Tent of Tomorrow's fiberglass roof, and weather destroyed the terrazzo tiles. In 2008, the

Tired of ancient ruins? Visit the wreckage of what
people thought the future would look like.

World Monument Fund added these structures to its endangered sites
list.

See the corroded skeletons at Flushing Meadows Corona Park
and check out Sam Rohn's panoramic photography at www.samrohn
.com/360-panorama/tent-of-tomorrow-1964-worlds-fair.

The Power of Babel

NYC is the most linguistically diverse city in the world. Some linguists estimate that New Yorkers speak eight hundred different languages. NYC public school students speak 176 languages. Residents of Queens, the most ethnically and linguistically diverse county in the US, listed 138 languages on their 2000 census forms.

Beware the Soup Dumpling

Nan Shian Dumpling House (Nan Xiang Xiao Long Bao)

Hapless Westerners often make fools of themselves by chowing down on a scalding soup dumpling. There's a trick to eating them, but before I reveal it, I'm sending you deep into Queens.

When most New Yorkers think of Chinatown, they think of the one straddling Canal Street in downtown Manhattan, not the Chinatown in Flushing, Queens. But in Flushing, you can sample a truly diverse selection of Chinese and Taiwanese foods at great prices, and parking is much easier and cheaper if you're traveling by car.

Xiao long bao (also known as soup dumplings or XLB) is an eastern Chinese dish from the Nan Shian suburb of Shanghai. The dumplings look like miniature pagodas, but inside the doughy wrapper, a crab or pork meatball basks in broth. They're called *xiao long bao*, or "little dumplings from basket," because they're traditionally steamed in a *xiaolong*, or "small steaming basket" made of bamboo.

Soup dumplings are extremely hard to do right: Ideally, the dough is diaphanous, yet thick enough to hold the soup. I haven't sampled all the soup dumplings in NYC, but my friend Pam swears by Nan

Watch the dumpling makers at Nan Shian Dumpling House.

Shian Dumpling House. Their dumplings are made to order, hence fresher than others in the neighborhood. You can watch the dumpling maker roll out your wrappers.

There's a trick to eating piping hot soup dumplings. If you bite into them immediately, the broth will scald your mouth. The trick is, first, to pick up the dumpling with tongs and place it in a soup spoon. Next, nibble on the dough to release the hot broth into the spoon. Finally, you can sip the broth from the spoon and eat the rest of the dumpling with chopsticks.

Nan Shian is located at 38-12 Prince Street between Thirty-Eighth and Thirty-Ninth Avenues. Call (718) 321-3838 for hours.

Tombstones beside a Parking Lot

As my friends and I left Nan Shian Dumpling House, we took a right on Prince and a left on Thirty-Ninth Avenue. Approaching Main Street, we stumbled upon some early nineteenth-century headstones lying in the dead leaves and trash next to a parking lot. As it turned out, we were around the corner from St. George's Episcopal Church. Though the current Neo-Gothic building was constructed in 1854, the church has been meeting since 1702 and now offers services in Chinese and Spanish as well as English.

Visit St. George's at 135-32 Thirty-Eighth Avenue, or at www .sg1702.org.

I never found out why these tombstones were separate from the rest of St. George's Cemetery.

Buy Peking Duck at a Window on the Street

The Corner 28 Restaurant

On Main Street in Flushing, you can walk up to a window on the street and buy Peking duck. This may not seem so special to us Americans, accustomed to ordering burgers at drive-thru windows, but Peking duck was traditionally a dish of emperors.

In 1330, the imperial court menu of the Yuan dynasty listed roast duck and described its preparation, but Peking duck was truly developed in the early 1400s, when the Ming dynasty moved its capital to Beijing. (Consequently, Peking duck is considered northern Chinese cuisine.) By the eighteenth century, the upper classes were enjoying the dish, but common people never got to taste it. The average Beijinger has only been able to afford Peking duck for the last ten years.

Sample the dish of emperors for $2.50 in Flushing.

★ ★

You can't make Peking duck at home. Chinese chefs insist that the skins must be dried then cooked in a brick oven over a real fire. None of this gas or electric hogwash.

The traditional Peking duck meal consists of three courses. First, you dine on the skin and fat, dipped in sugar and garlic. Then you eat the meat in a pancake with plum sauce, leeks, and cucumber. Whatever is left goes into a soup.

The ducks get the short end of the deal. They're free-range for the first forty-five days of their lives, but then they're force-fed for twenty days before they're slaughtered. I usually refrain—in solidarity with the ducks—but at the Corner 28 window on Main Street, I tried a small portion of Peking duck in a pancake for $2.50. It was delicious.

But—before anyone gets too cocky—while you may be able to buy Peking duck through a window in Flushing, Beijingers say you can't get authentic Peking duck anywhere but in Beijing.

Corner 28 is open daily from 8:30 a.m. to 1:00 a.m. at 40-28 Main Street in Flushing. Call (718) 886-6628.

Bubble Tea
Quickly

Imagine sipping sweet, milky iced tea through a straw. Suddenly, a Gummi Bear shoots into your mouth.

If you haven't spent much time in East Asia—or in a large, bustling Chinatown—you're in for a surprise with bubble tea. The "bubbles" aren't Gummi Bears, but rubbery, black, gumball-size tapioca pearls that you sip through a wide straw and chew. Swallowing them whole is not recommended, and inhaling will probably ruin the experience.

Bubble tea first appeared in Taiwan in the early 1980s. It then migrated to mainland China, the Philippines, and Singapore, crossed the Pacific to Vancouver, Canada, then popped up in Chinatown areas of New York and other U.S. cities.

The most popular bubble tea is pearl milk tea or boba milk tea—a

全球最大
珍珠奶茶
WORLD BIGGEST
BUBBLE TEA
JUICE & SLUSH

It takes a while to get used to sipping
tapioca balls through a straw.

mixture of black tea, milk, and boba balls, made from tapioca and
carrageenan powder—but many variants contain fruit or fruit syrup.

Quickly bills itself as the "World [*sic*] Largest Bubble Tea" franchise.
I'd rather plug local independent stores than franchises, but Quickly
makes a great bubble tea, as does Ten Ren—another chain that has a
location on Roosevelt Street in Flushing.

Quickly is located at 41-40 Kissena Boulevard in Flushing. Call (718)
358-1835.

★ ★

Trivia

Before a 1978 law required New Yorkers to clean up after their pets, dogs deposited an annual forty million pounds of feces onto the streets.

Manhattan Loses Civic Virtue to Queens
Civic Virtue Fountain

During the 1920s and 1930s, Manhattan's most embarrassing monument was Civic Virtue, a fountain prominently displayed in City Hall Park. The twenty-foot marble sculpture featured a naked man, representing Virtue, stomping on two mermaids who—according to sculptor Frederick MacMonnies—represented Vice. Unveiled in 1922, the statue immediately sparked protest and was nicknamed "Rough Guy."

This major faux pas was a classic example of municipal bureaucracy lagging behind social and legal change. Angelina Crane bequeathed NYC money to build a fountain in 1891, but the city took until 1909 to commission the sculptor, and MacMonnies didn't complete his design until 1919. By the time the fountain was unveiled, it was 1922. American women had been granted suffrage after a long campaign, and they saw the injustice they'd been fighting against embodied in the statue of the man trampling women right in front of City Hall.

Despite public outcry, Rough Guy stood his ground in City Hall Park for nineteen years. Apparently, the statue's butt crack faced the municipal building's entrance, and mayor Fiorello La Guardia got sick of being mooned every day when he left work. He finally figured out a way to get rid of it. In 1941, he "regifted" the fountain to Queens in honor of the opening of their Borough Hall. Thanks a lot, Manhattan.

Today, Rough Guy remains a "butt" of feminist critique. He's simply less obtrusive—located at Queens Boulevard and Union Turnpike.

Mayor La Guardia tired of seeing Rough Guy's butt crack and gave the fountain to Queens.

7

The Bronx

Seventy years ago, the mere mention of the Bronx provoked laughter. The borough was strongly associated with a noise of disapproval, the Bronx cheer—also known as blowing a raspberry, or in technical terms, an unvoiced linguolabial trill. Bronx borough president James J. Lyons spent most of his twenty-eight-year tenure trying to get people to stop laughing when they heard the word Bronx. "The so-called Bronx cheer," Lyons would tell the papers, "is a noise brought to the Bronx, especially to the Yankee Stadium, by vulgar people from outside the Bronx." Long-suffering Bronx natives simply had to tolerate baseball fans farting with their mouths. What were they to do? Kick them out of the ballpark?

Arriving at the Bronx and Staten Island, we come upon a new category—ambivalent boroughs, boroughs that are less than thrilled to be one of the five. If we look at NYC as one big dysfunctional family, the Bronx has been a bit standoffish, while Staten Island has actually sued for divorce. Queens, Brooklyn, and Manhattan have their complaints, but the relations seem a bit less fraught.

Between 1950 and 1980, the South Bronx went into economic freefall, partly because NYC's master builder, Robert Moses, plowed a highway through a densely populated urban area: The Cross Bronx Expressway uprooted thousands and devastated residential

* *

neighborhoods—culminating in waves of arson. As property values plummeted, landlords set their buildings on fire, collected insurance, and left behind a series of burnt-out shells.

The South Bronx has bounced back since the 1980s, largely due to the work of grassroots organizations like Nos Quedamos (www.nosquedamos.org), which forced the city to include residents of the Melrose Commons area in urban planning. Today the Bronx is better known for Yankee Stadium and the Bronx Zoo than for arson and farting noises.

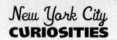
★ ★

Tropical Oasis in the South Bronx
La Casita Rincón Criollo

What would it take to evoke the tropical Puerto Rican countryside in densely urban New York? A heated dome with a HEPA filter and sprinkler system? Community groups in the Bronx and East Harlem have conjured rural Puerto Rico by building casitas with scrapwood and found objects.

A casita is a "little house"—commonly found in preindustrial Puerto Rico—with a low roof and a deck surrounded by a *batey* (a yard without grass) and vegetable gardens. In the Bronx and East Harlem, casitas function as clubhouses for hanging out, urban gardening, and social events with Puerto Rican traditions like *bomba* and *plena*. (*Bomba* is a lively dialogue of rhythm and movement between drummers and dancers. Originating in sixteenth-century Africa, it first served to call tribes to meeting and later to organize slave revolts. *Plena*, with Spanish and West African roots, is called *el periódica cantado*, "the sung newspaper," because its lyrics contain local gossip, news, and political commentary.)

One of the oldest casitas in the South Bronx is La Casita Rincón Criollo. Roughly translated as "Down-Home Corner," Rincón Criollo dates back to the late 1970s, when the South Bronx was devastated by arson and poverty. Inspired by a casita he'd seen in East Harlem, José (Chema) Soto started picking up garbage in a vacant, city-owned lot he passed every day. His neighbors pitched in, and soon a community formed to turn this patch of unkempt land into a neighborhood garden and gathering place.

Since the city still owned the land, Rincón Criollo faced numerous threats of eviction. In 2007, the casita moved a block south to make way for low-income housing. Today the casita features a two-room, blue-green clubhouse, a clean-swept yard, lush vegetable gardens enclosed in bright yellow fences, a shrine to the Virgin, a scarecrow, a Port-a-Potty, and lots of children's toys.

Members say the casita truly feels like Puerto Rico. With a bamboo

La Casita Rincón Criollo puts the Puerto Rican countryside
in the South Bronx.
BOBBY MORGAN

floor, an outhouse, and people whistling like the *coquí*, a small frog
endemic to Puerto Rico, Rincón Criollo helps members navigate the
chasm between the Puerto Rican and American ways of life and helps
them teach their children how to deal with those differences as well.

Everyone is welcome at La Casita Rincón Criollo, located at East
157th Street and Brook Avenue in Melrose. Find La Casita online at
www.myspace.com/rinconcriollo.

★ ★

Hip-Hop Stars Give History Tours

Hush Tours

Think of a particular genre of music—rock, jazz, classical. Can you pinpoint the exact address and date where it started? Probably not.

In the early 1970s, hip-hop was emerging in several places—in the Bronx, Harlem, Brooklyn, and Queens. But pioneers and historians say that major developments took place in the West Bronx at the free parties in the rec room of 1520 Sedgwick Avenue: DJ Kool Herc, a Jamaican immigrant named Clive Campbell, started "break" spinning. By switching back and forth between two copies of the same record on two separate turntables, he prolonged the instrumental (percussion) solo in a song to give people more time to dance. Breakdancing emerged along with the break beat. And while the b-boys and b-girls were breakdancing, MC Coke La Rock rapped in the tradition of Jamaican sound-system toasts.

In 2007, the New York State Office of Parks, Recreation, and Historic Preservation dubbed 1520 Sedgwick Avenue the Birthplace of Hip-Hop. Some people even claim that DJ Kool Herc threw the first true hip-hop party at 1520 Sedgwick on August 11, 1973.

Now, DJ Kool Herc works for Hush Tours as a celebrity guide along with a number of other hip-hop luminaries and pioneers, like Grandmaster Caz of Cold Crush Brothers, DJ Red Alert, Kurtis Blow (whose 1980 single "The Breaks" was the first gold rap record), Rahiem of Grandmaster Flash and the Furious Five, Reggie Reg of Crash Crew, Ralph McDaniels, and Mickey D of Main Source. Guides show off hip-hop landmarks, reminisce about the early days, and play music on the bus, including early rap records like the first rap single, the Fatback Band's "King Tim III (Personality Jock)."

Debra Harris founded Hush Tours in 2002, because hip-hop had lifted her spirits while she was growing up in the Bronx. She started giving spontaneous tours to her children, because she wanted to pass on the heritage and give them some of the experiences she'd had. She soon discovered a niche market.

Hush Tours started with the "birthplace of hip-hop" tour of Harlem and the Bronx and has expanded to Brooklyn and Queens. The bus leaves from Midtown. Visit www.hushtours.com for tour times.

Forgotten Fame
Hall of Fame for Great Americans

Ever heard of the Cockroach Hall of Fame, founded by a pest-control specialist in Plano, Texas? It features "Liberoachi" and other dead bugs dressed as celebrities. How about the Cricket Hall of Fame—for the sport, not the insect? Or the All-American Soap Box Derby Hall of Fame in Akron, Ohio?

Who started this Hall of Fame business anyway?

King Ludwig of Bavaria, who had a penchant for building fantasy castles, erected two Halls of Fame (*Ruhmeshalle* in German) in the mid-1800s and crowned them with statues of his favorite Teutonic luminaries. In the 1890s, the chancellor of New York University (NYU) decided his new campus in the Bronx needed a Hall of Fame, too. He had Stanford White design a 630-foot open-air colonnade to honor "Great Americans," whose bronze busts would bedeck the hall. This American Hall of Fame had to be slightly more democratic than King Ludwig's—but not *too* democratic. While anyone could nominate Great Americans who had been dead for twenty-five years,

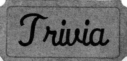

Trivia

In New York State, it is illegal for a man to turn around on a city street and look at a woman "in that way." After a second conviction, the violator will be forced to wear horse blinders.

★ ★

the chancellor appointed one hundred electors to ensure that his hall wasn't decorated with famous burlesque dancers of the day.

The Hall of Fame for Great Americans opened in 1900. For several decades, Hall of Famers ranked above Nobel Laureates. But gradually the idea of fame changed. Fewer people believed in universal great- ness or in "great men" who somehow transcended their place and time the way Roman emperors supposedly attained godlike status. Nonetheless, people still thought it worth recognizing achievement in

Halls of Fame aren't just for the likes of Lincoln anymore. Now even dead cockroaches have a chance.

particular fields, like baseball, basketball, and insurance sales. So Halls of Fame arose for nearly everything, including cockroaches.

Today, the Hall of Fame for Great Americans seems starkly disconnected from the largely Latino Bronx Community College—and from the Bronx. Of ninety-eight honorees, none is Latino, Asian, or Native American. Only two are black, two are Jewish, and eleven are women.

Ironically, with only eleven busts of women, the Hall of Fame has more monuments to historical women than all five boroughs combined. NYC statuary features a host of allegorical and mythological matrons and maidens—Lady Liberty, Minerva, Africa, Asia, Europa— but only five statues of women who actually walked the Earth: Joan of Arc, Gertrude Stein, Eleanor Roosevelt, Golda Meir, and Harriet Tubman. None of the statues in Central Park honors a real woman— only Alice in Wonderland and Mother Goose.

Located in Bronx Community College (BCC) at University Avenue and West 181st Street, the Hall of Fame is free to the public and open daily from 10:00 a.m. to 5:00 p.m. To schedule a tour, call (718) 289-5161 or (718) 289-5877, or take the virtual tour at www.bcc.cuny .edu/halloffame/#.

The Raven's Perch
Edgar Allan Poe Cottage

Are you a goth chick seeking summer employment? How about live-in caretaker at the Poe Cottage? Stop vandals from smashing windows. Keep cyberpunk scientists from collecting DNA samples for cloning experiments.

Today, the quaint clapboard house where Poe wrote "Annabel Lee," "The Bells," and "Eureka" squats next to the heavily trafficked Grand Concourse with Art Deco apartment buildings looming overhead.

But in 1846—when Fordham was still bucolic farmland—Poe, his wife Virginia Clemm, and her mother rented the humble cottage on

You could be the next live-in caretaker at the Edgar Allan Poe cottage.

the corner of 192nd Street and Kingsbridge Road. Poe hoped the fresh air would cure Virginia of tuberculosis, but she died on January 30, 1847.

Poe Cottage is filled with period furniture. The table is set as if Poe might show up for lunch. A quill lies on the parlor desk, though Poe supposedly displayed his wife in her coffin there.

Unfortunately, it isn't Poe's actual desk. After his mysterious death in 1849, his mother-in-law, Maria Clemm, sold his furniture to the neighbors, who handed it down from generation to generation, until someone finally donated a few pieces to the Poe Cottage: a mirror, Poe's rocking chair, and Virginia's deathbed.

★ ★

Around 1900, it looked as if the house would be torn down to make way for development. But in 1913, the New York Shakespeare Society bought it and moved it into the park, so the quaint cottage now stands on a patch of grass, next to the bustling Grand Concourse.

The relocation seems appropriate, since Poe himself was nomadic—living intermittently in Philadelphia, Baltimore, and NYC. In NYC alone, he resided on Waverly Place, Carmine Street, Greenwich Street, Amity (now West Third) Street, Broadway, Bond Street, Eighty-Fourth Street, and in what is now the Poe Cottage.

The Poe Cottage, located at 2640 Grand Concourse, is undergoing major restoration in 2010 and 2011. While the site is closed for renovation, visit the Poe exhibit at the Valentine-Varian House at 3266 Bainbridge Avenue and East 208th Street. Museum hours are Saturday from 10:00 a.m. to 4:00 p.m. and Sunday from 1:00 p.m. to 5:00 p.m. Check www.bronxhistoricalsociety.org/poecottage.html for updates, or call the Bronx Historical Society at (718) 881-8900 for tour information.

Poe-hemia

"Before Poe, the artistic life in New York was genteel and respectably settled into the social order," writes Luc Santé in *Low Life*. Washington Irving dreamed up a headless horseman, but he won literary renown at age twenty-six and made a hearty living with his pen until he died fifty years later.

The depressed, alcoholic Poe, by contrast, drifted—unrecognized and despised—from one shabby rental to another. In 1845, the publication of his poem "The Raven" brought him instant fame, but he still worked fourteen-hour days and couldn't earn a living. He died at age forty of unknown causes—probably after a long bender.

After Poe's death, it became fashionable to emulate his misery. Certainly, artists suffered in obscurity before Poe, but Poe's poverty, immense suffering, overnight fame, and early death seemed to spawn legions of Bohemians, tortured artists, eccentric idealists living like

★ ★

church mice, sacrificing health and happiness for art, and burning themselves out in a blaze of manic ambition and recklessness.

While Poe's characters were often mad and depraved, there's little evidence that their author was. Unfortunately, Poe's envious literary executor, Rufus Wilmot Griswold, portrayed him as a wicked and drug-addled maniac, forged crazy letters, and attributed them to Poe as proof of his derangements. Though the letters were later found to be forgeries, the notion of Poe as a mad, evil genius titillated readers so much that it became part of the Poe mystique.

The Bronx Is Gneiss, but Manhattan Is a Piece of Schist

The Riverdale and Grand Concourse ridges in the Bronx consist of billion-year-old Fordham Gneiss—a type of rock transformed by pressure and heat.

The backbone of Manhattan Island consists of schist—a different kind of metamorphic rock, seen most clearly in Central Park's crags and boulders. Roughly 450 million years ago, lava spewed through the earth's crust and hardened into an arc of volcanic islands off the northeast coast of the early North American continent. Over hundreds of millions of years, intense heat and pressure converted volcanic ash into schist, and the arc of volcanic islands became what we know as Manhattan, as continents colliding and scraping over each other folded and twisted layers of schist, marble, and gneiss into the Manhattan bedrock.

Disputed Land

Marble Hill

The Bronx is the only borough that lies primarily on the mainland, not on an island. I say *primarily* because a tiny peninsula attached to Manhattan Island is technically part of the Bronx, while a neighborhood on the mainland is part of Manhattan.

Before 1895, the winding Spuyten Duyvil Creek separated Manhattan Island from the mainland. The creek made a loop around a neighborhood known as Marble Hill, which was connected to Manhattan.

This map depicts Spuyten Duyvil Creek over 115 years ago, before the Harlem River Ship Canal. Marble Hill was part of Manhattan Island, and a little peninsula was linked to the mainland.

★ ★

Trivia

In New York State, you may be fined $25 for flirting.

But in the late 1800s, the U.S. Army Corps of Engineers started altering the creek and surrounding land: They sliced Marble Hill off from Manhattan to create the Harlem River Ship Canal, allowing large vessels to pass more easily between the Hudson and Harlem Rivers. Spuyten Duyvil Creek still bordered Marble Hill's north, east, and west, but the Harlem River Ship Canal now lay to the south, making Marble Hill an island.

In 1912, New York State divided NYC into five counties. Most of the county lines followed waterways. But Marble Hill residents insisted they lived in Manhattan (New York County). Even after 1914, when the state filled in the stretch of Spuyten Duyvil Creek that separated Marble Hill from the mainland, Marble Hill refused to belong to the Bronx.

The territorial battle carried on—peaking in 1939, when Bronx borough president James J. Lyons planted the Bronx flag on a rocky crag in Marble Hill and claimed it as the "Bronx Sudetenland." The previous year, Hitler had seized the Sudetenland—Czechoslovakia's western edge—in his quest for German expansion. Lyons' mock invasion was unsuccessful, and we can all be thankful that the Bronx didn't repeat the history of Nazi Germany.

Today, Marble Hill is still officially part of Manhattan: Its residents vote in Manhattan, but their fire, police, school, and emergency medical services come from the Bronx. Since traffic bottlenecks around bridges, Marble Hill residents don't mind being part of the Bronx when their houses catch fire, or when they're choking on a chicken bone or being mugged.

Spuyten Duyvil Creek and Shorefront Park

The British were threatening to attack New Amsterdam on a stormy night in 1664. Dutch director-general Peter Stuyvesant dispatched an envoy, Antony Van Corlear, to ride to the mainland and blast his trumpet, rousing the Dutch settlers for war.

But when Antony reached the creek dividing Manhattan from what is now the Bronx, the water was too swollen to cross. Vowing to "swim across in spite of the devil (*spyt den duyvel*)," Antony plunged into the swirling waters, according to Washington Irving's satirical *History of New-York* (1809).

The devil took the dare. Antony had struggled halfway across the creek, when an enormous fish—which eyewitnesses identified as the devil—seized his leg. The trumpeter blew his horn as loud as he could before he sank to the bottom. "The place," wrote Irving, "has been called Spyt den Duyvel ever since; the ghost of the unfortunate Antony still haunts the surrounding solitudes, and his trumpet has often been heard by the neighbors on a stormy night, mingling with the howling of the blast."

But apparently, Antony didn't drown. He waded across Spuyten Duyvil Creek, according to W. H. Shelton, curator of the Morris-Jumel Mansion, who found the story in a soldier's journal.

No one knows for sure where the name Spuyten Duyvil comes from. It may mean "devil's whirlpool" or "spouting devil" (*spuitende duivel* in contemporary Dutch). Though this moniker makes the creek sound treacherous, the water was supposedly so shallow that people used to wade across it to avoid paying ferry tolls.

Irving's devilish tale caught on because he engaged in some wily stealth marketing before publishing his satire. Pretending to be a hotel owner, he contacted local newspapers and placed missing persons notices for Diedrich Knickerbocker, a curmudgeonly Dutch historian, who had gone missing from his hotel without paying the bill. If Knickerbocker didn't come back and settle his accounts, the hotel owner vowed he'd publish a manuscript the historian had left behind.

★ ★

Trivia

On the Wild Asia Monorail at the Bronx Zoo, you'll find yourself in a cage while the animals run wild. Call it a zoo in reverse.

The hoax caught on, and Irving soon published his history—under the pen name Diedrich Knickerbocker—to great acclaim.

Follow the footpaths around Spuyten Duyvil Shorefront Park for some glorious views of Inwood Hill Park—with a Metro-North station and the underside of the Hudson Bridge thrown in.

Spuyten Duyvil Shorefront Park offers magnificent views of Spuyten Duyvil Creek and Inwood Hill Park. If you hear a clarion call, it's probably not Antony Van Corlear, who survived Spuyten Duyvil.

Cemetery Monument Takes a Dive
Bronx River Soldier

For more than six decades, an unmarked statue of a Civil War soldier stood "at ease" on a pedestal in the middle of the Bronx River, just south of East Gun Hill Road. In a long coat and a Union Army kepi, the gray-granite soldier leaned pensively on his musket—in clear view of the Bronx River Parkway. Highway drivers spotted the statue and wondered: Where did he come from? What was he doing in the middle of the river? Some people died wondering. Local histories and guidebooks gave no clues.

In 1964, the soldier finally leaned forward and toppled face first into the water. The New York City Parks Department staged a dramatic rescue then stored the monument in a warehouse until someone figured out what to do with it. In 1970, they installed the statue outside the Bronx County Historical Society's office in the colonial Valentine-Varian House.

As it turned out, a veterans' group commissioned John Grignoloa to sculpt this statue for the Grand Army of the Republic (GAR) burial plot in Woodlawn Cemetery. But the statue got chipped, and the GAR rejected it.

A few years later, John B. Lazzari, who owned a local gravestone quarry, saw the statue in Grignoloa's studio, took a liking to it, and displayed it on his lawn on the Bronx River's west bank, just south of Gun Hill Road. Lazzari also had a footbridge, supported by a granite pier. When local workers started using the wooden bridge as a shortcut to the tapestry factory on the east bank, Lazzari tore it down—leaving only a granite pier in the middle of the river.

At some point in 1898, Lazzari tired of the soldier on his lawn. He installed the statue on the granite pier and carved 1898 into the base. There, in the middle of the Bronx River, the soldier stood sentry for sixty-six years and piqued the curiosity of passers-by, until he finally keeled over.

At the Valentine-Varian House, located at 3266 Bainbridge Avenue

★ ★

at East 208th Street, you can still visit the Bronx River Soldier—an exemplary Civil War monument, modeled on John Quincy Adams Ward's Seventh Regiment Memorial overlooking the West Loop in Central Park. But you have to imagine him taking a dive.

The Bronx River Soldier was once a lawn ornament. Some people like gnomes or pink flamingos, while others prefer cemetery monuments.
BOBBY MORGAN

8

Staten Island

From 1948 to *2001, Staten Island claimed that the other four boroughs treated it like trash. This wasn't just a metaphor. Every day, NYC
dumped all its municipal waste onto the Fresh Kills Landfill in Staten
Island. The 2,200-acre trash heap was perhaps the largest human-made
structure on Earth. It could be seen from space.*

*This wasn't the first time the "Forgotten Borough" found itself on the
wrong side of NYC, or on the wrong side of history. In 1858, New York
built a quarantine hospital on Staten Island for immigrants who had
just arrived at Ellis Island and been diagnosed with contagious diseases.
Irate Staten Islanders ran the patients from the hospital and burned the
building down.*

*Earlier, during the Revolutionary War, the isolated, rural population
of Staten Island was overwhelmingly loyal to the crown. George Washington called them "cruel and unrelenting enemies."*

*Staten Island played a pivotal role in the war, due to its strategic
position at the entrance to the New York Harbor. In the summer of
1776, as the British prepared to invade New York, which then consisted
only of the southern tip of Manhattan, more than 140 British ships
anchored off the shores of Staten Island. An armada this large would
not set sail again until World War II. It's hard to underestimate the terror New Yorkers must have felt, gazing across the harbor at the British
fleet—undisputed master of the seven seas—ready to attack.*

British general William Howe set up his headquarters on Staten

Island at the Rose and Crown Tavern near the present-day junction of Richmond Road and New Dorp Lane. A boulder now marks this spot, where Howe first learned of the Declaration of Independence. The British offered peace—on condition that the Patriots withdraw the statement. On September 11, 1776, three Very Important Patriots—Benjamin Franklin, John Adams, and Edward Rutledge—met with the British at the now-famous conference house on Staten Island (www .conferencehouse.org). I don't have to tell you that the meeting didn't end in peace.

More than two hundred years later, Staten Island is much less rural, but still NYC's most suburban borough. With fewer than 500,000 residents, its population is still smaller than Manhattan's was in 1850. You'll find out more about the Fresh Kills Landfill in this chapter, but basically the city shut it down. So Staten Island no longer has to think of itself as the municipal trash bin.

In 1905, when the city took over the operation of the Staten Island Ferry, livestock rode alongside human passengers.

Secession

In 1993, Staten Islanders voted to secede from NYC. The five boroughs had been together since 1898, when Staten Island, Brooklyn, Queens, and the eastern part of the Bronx were incorporated into the City of New York, which previously included only Manhattan and the West Bronx. But the union was fraught, as far as Staten Island was concerned. Chief complaint was the Fresh Kills Landfill. How would you feel if each day the city dumped thirteen thousand tons of municipal waste on you? Moreover, the ferry cost fifty cents. With all the garbage they had to deal with, Staten Islanders wanted a free ride.

If the divorce had succeeded, Staten Island would have been the second-largest city in New York State, but the State Assembly blocked implementation.

John J. Marchi, the freedom fighter who led the movement for Staten Island's secession in the New York State Senate, died in April 2009. His vision of deliverance survives in his successor, Andrew J. Lanza. But overall, Staten Islanders are happier, now that Fresh Kills Landfill is closed and they can ride the ferry for free.

Incidentally, Staten Islanders aren't the first to press for secession. In 1950, Norman Mailer ran for mayor on the platform that all of New York City should secede from New York State.

★ ★

I Shouldn't Have to Tell You to Take the Ferry
St. George Terminal

The Staten Island Ferry may seem too commonplace for a book of strange and funny sites. But I'm always shocked at how many New Yorkers and frequent tourists have never set foot on the ferry—especially since it's free and offers panoramic views of the Statue of Liberty and New York Harbor.

You don't get these kinds of views on the subway. Yet, the ferry only carries sixty thousand riders per weekday, while the subway transports five million—winning the popularity contest by a long shot. Of course, the subway also has 468 station stops, while the ferry has only two. But plainly we all need to find new jobs on Staten Island, if we want a more scenic commute.

Here's a twilight view of the St. George Ferry Terminal from a Manhattan-bound ferry.

Waiting for the ferry has also gotten much more fun, since the St. George Ferry Terminal had a makeover. The brick wall facing the harbor has been replaced with a forty-foot-tall glass wall, so passengers waiting inside the terminal can see the ferry coming. The spectacular fish tanks earn their own entry below.

Catch the ferry at the Whitehall Terminal near Battery Park in Lower Manhattan. The 5.2-mile trip lasts twenty-five minutes each way, and even though the ride is free, you can't stay on roundtrip. You have to disembark at each terminal and go through the turnstile. (This discourages people from living on the ferry.) You can get back on the same boat, but why not venture outside the terminal and take a look around Staten Island first?

A final word about ferry crashes: Such accidents get lots of news coverage partly because they're so rare. The ferry remains the safest form of mass transit—and the most reliable. It's punctual 96 percent of the time.

St. George Ferry Terminal is located at 1 Bay Street. Check out the website, www.siferry.com, for schedules, photos of current and past ferries, and other fun stuff.

A Modern-Day "Cabinet of Curiosities"
Staten Island Museum

What contains the rind of a four-pound lemon, a solid baseball-size hairball from a cow's stomach, a 1940s matchbox filled with rabbit feces, and a pickled four-legged chicken, dated January 1, 1914?

Answer: The Display of Strange Things at the Staten Island Museum.

Founded in 1881, the Staten Island Museum proudly describes its oddest exhibit, the Hall of Natural Science, as its very own "cabinet of curiosities." In Renaissance Europe, some kings, aristocrats, and scientists assembled cabinets of curiosities, or "wonder-rooms," filled with preserved animals, rocks, shells, seemingly mythical creatures, and other objects that defied classification. Similarly, the Staten Island

Museum boasts a collection of stuffed birds and mammals, dinosaur footprints, fluorescent minerals, and jars of random specimens preserved in formaldehyde, and a striking 120-year-old Victorian shadow box—jammed with a mink chomping on a chicken's neck, a squirrel gnawing on an acorn, and countless other animals and insects united in a proximity that would never be found in nature. I was disappointed that I couldn't take photographs.

In addition to the Hall of Natural Science, visitors can enjoy rotating history and art exhibits, and the Wall of Insects—highlights from the museum's collection of more than five hundred thousand defunct butterflies, cicadas, and beetles. An entomologist's and a taxidermist's dream.

On a more serious, but no less interesting note, the museum has a permanent installation of Lenape Indian artifacts, including pieces from the Paleoindians, the first people who inhabited the land now known as NYC 11,000 years ago.

The Staten Island Museum at 75 Stuyvesant Place is a short walk from the St. George's Ferry Terminal. Visit from noon to 5:00 p.m. Sunday through Friday, 10:00 a.m. to 5:00 p.m. Saturday, or on the web at www.StatenIslandMuseum.org. Call (718) 727-1135 for more information.

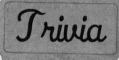

Trivia

In NYC, the penalty for jumping off of a building is death.

A Whale of the Fish Tank

Two eight-foot tall, two-thousand-gallon saltwater fish tanks stand in the middle of the terminal. Each holds two hundred tropical fish, protected by three-inch-thick acrylic glass. Beams beneath the floor support the ten-ton tanks.

Be sure to bring your camera. While you're waiting for the ferry, everyone around you will be flashing their cameras at the fish, and you won't want to miss out.

The fish don't seem to mind the constant flash photography.

★ ★

Antonio Meucci: Neglected Telephone Inventor
Garibaldi-Meucci Museum

Before we could purchase a dial tone that made our cell phone quack like a duck or moo like a cow, our telephones rang like bells. This made it easy to remember that Alexander Graham Bell invented the telephone.

But what if he didn't? Like most technological innovations, the telephone was the culmination of many inventors' work. In fact, telephone history is littered with more than six hundred lawsuits. After securing the master patent and getting all the credit, Bell spent most of his time in court.

The first to produce a working device may have been the Italian-born inventor Antonio Meucci. In 1850, Meucci and his wife, Esther, immigrated to the United States and settled in Staten Island, where he eked out a living making smokeless candles in a small backyard furnace. By 1857, he had constructed a device that allowed him to communicate with his wife, Esther, at a distance—while he was working in the backyard and she was bedridden with arthritis on the second floor. Meucci couldn't afford large-scale demonstrations or a patent application. Financiers paid to patent some of his simpler inventions, but it was harder to explain how the *teletrofono* worked, and Meucci didn't speak English. In 1871, he filed a patent caveat, which described the "sound telegraph" he intended to patent and temporarily prevented the patent office from granting anyone else a patent for that invention. He couldn't scrape together the $10 to renew his caveat in 1874. Bell secured the master patent two years later.

Meucci sued but lost. He couldn't afford a decent lawyer, while Bell's father-in-law, the powerful financier Gardiner Greene Hubbard, had organized the Bell Telephone Company and had an interest in its success. Moreover, Esther had sold the working *teletrofoni* models to pay bills while Meucci was hospitalized following an 1871 ferryboat explosion.

In 2002, the U.S. House of Representatives passed a resolution

Nestore Corradi drew this illustration of Meucci's model in 1858. Note the caption, "Electric current from the inductor pipe."
COURTESY OF THE GARIBALDI-MEUCCI MUSEUM

stating, "If Meucci had been able to pay the $10 fee to maintain the caveat after 1874, no patent could have been issued to Bell." This didn't settle the matter. Ten days later, the Canadian government passed a motion affirming that Alexander Graham Bell invented the telephone.

At 420 Tompkins Avenue, you can visit Meucci's house and see his inventions, including a few of his many *teletrofoni* designs. The house was preserved because the Meuccis took in the Italian war hero Giuseppe Garibaldi. Meucci himself is almost unknown. Visit the museum from 1:00 p.m. to 5:00 p.m. Tuesday through Sunday or on the web at www.garibaldimeuccimuseum.org. Call (718) 442-1608 for more info.

Unifier of Italy, Candlemaker in Staten Island

Giuseppe Garibaldi, a rather complex and paradoxical political figure, was dubbed Hero of the Two Worlds for his military exploits in Brazil, Uruguay, and France and for his later role in the unification of Italy. In 1860, his army of one thousand captured the island of Sicily, then invaded the mainland and occupied Naples in an effort to unify the Italian peninsula. These attempts to unite Italy were lionized in the Civil War–torn United States. Abraham Lincoln was so impressed that, in 1862, he offered the Italian general command of the Union forces. Garibaldi said yes—but only if Lincoln would abolish slavery. Lincoln refused. In 1862, he feared that freeing the slaves would worsen a national agricultural crisis.

In the early 1850s, before his unification campaign, Garibaldi lived in Staten Island. Italian inventor Antonio Meucci and his wife, Esther, welcomed the exiled Garibaldi into their home, where he stayed sporadically for several years—helping Meucci manufacture smokeless candles and generally maintaining a low profile.

Garibaldi, taken in Naples, Italy. 1861.
LIBRARY OF CONGRESS

★ ★

Tiki Staten Island

Jade Island

Tiki bars have little to do with Polynesian cultures or the carved-wood humanoid figures called tikis that mark the borders of sacred sites. But in the mid-1930s, American entrepreneurs figured out they could make a chunk of change by decking cocktail lounges and eateries with snarling tiki heads, thatch huts, fake volcanoes, puffer fish lamps, and bamboo, and serving Asian-fusion cuisine and tropical drinks.

Staten Island's very own vintage tiki restaurant, Jade Island, is located in a strip mall with a Pathmark and Kmart. The menu offers Cantonese, Szechuan, and Polynesian dishes. The cocktail menu features photos of drinks, so you can see if your mai tai, zombie, or headhunter will be served in a fresh coconut shell, pineapple rind, or tiki mug. All drinks seem to include the requisite paper umbrella.

Jade Island has thrived since the strip mall opened in 1969. I doubt the decor has changed much. Loyal customers rave about the reasonably priced, hearty portions and delicious drinks. I found the food a bit greasy and the drinks syrupy, but the ornamentation is truly over-the-top. The reception area boasts a backlit 3-D waterfall scene, plastic palm trees, gold Buddha, garish seahorse lamp, and lotto-ticket counter. In the dining room, you can sip your mai tai in a faux bamboo hut booth beside a yellow-tinted, backlit mural of Tahiti with gentle waves, sailboats, palm trees, and volcanic mountains. Starfish and puffer fish lamps abound. Requisite wooden tikis stand in the back near the kitchen beside a calculator for waiters to add up the bill. The tikis aren't guarding a sacred site, but they keep customers from inadvertently wandering into the kitchen.

Visit Jade Island at 2845 Richmond Avenue (between Yukon and Independence Avenues) Sunday through Thursday from 11:30 a.m. to 11:30 p.m., Friday from 11:30 a.m. to 12:30 a.m., or Saturday from 12:30 p.m. to 12:30 a.m.

Along this span of Richmond Avenue, it's easy to get lost in a series of seemingly endless strip malls—especially if you assume the parking lots are interlinked and look for passageways from one to the

Jade Island is your ticket to tiki dining—with bamboo booths, snarling tiki heads, puffer fish lamps, fake volcanoes, and waterfalls.

next. This is a trap for fools. Trust the towering KMART sign to lead you to the correct strip mall. When you turn into the parking lot, Jade Island will be on your left near Sleepy's and to the right of a post office. Call (718) 761-8080 for more info, or if you're really lost.

Historic Richmond Town

In Historic Richmond Town, NYC's only restored museum village, costumed role players recreate the lives of ordinary Staten Islanders from colonial times through the present day in buildings dating back as far as the 1690s. It's like Colonial Williamsburg, but less than twenty miles from Manhattan.

Almost all the structures in Historic Richmond Town are original, rather than reconstructed. Some buildings were moved to their present location by numbering each of the stones. Early Dutch settlers built the Voorlezer's House at its present site before 1696; it remains the oldest surviving schoolhouse in the United States. The general store, circa 1840, is full of early twentieth-century items. From 1880 to 1918, three sisters, Mary, Sarah, and Josephine Black, owned and operated the store. The sisters had a tacit agreement that none of them would ever marry: According to the laws of the day, if one of the sisters wed, the store would belong entirely to her new husband, and all three women would lose ownership.

At the time I'm writing, Historic Richmond Town is open Wednesday through Sunday, and located at 441 Clarke Avenue. In July and August, and on selected days throughout year, the museum "guarantees a historical living experience"—which means you'll run into some folks in period costumes practicing traditional trades like blacksmithing and basket weaving.

Some of the best offerings are for kids. What did you want to be when you grew up? An artist? A doctor? How about a tinsmith? In a two-week intensive summer program, eleven- to fourteen-year-olds can dress in period clothes and apprentice under a master tinsmith, cook, or basket maker. It's great career prep for kids who want to become historical re-enactors.

Annie in the
Tinsmith Shop;
Norm by the
Cooper Shop.
Many staff
members began
their careers
as apprentices
when they
were eleven
or twelve.

★ ★

For kids in grades three through six, the museum offers spooky sleepovers in the courtroom where Polly Bodine stood trial for the grisly murder of her sister-in-law and baby niece in 1843. The evening features a dramatic retelling of the trial, and the kids get to decide the verdict.

Visit www.historicrichmondtown.org on the web, or call (718) 351-1611 ext. 280 for detailed hours and more information.

Polly Bodine, "The Witch of Staten Island"

Polly Bodine isn't a household name these days, but she was legendary in 1843 when she stood trial for the murder of her sister-in-law and baby niece. The evidence pointed to Polly, but she had no chance of a fair trial. Since she was a "fallen woman," who had separated from her husband and had an extramarital affair and an abortion, the newspapers presumed her guilty and had a heyday with the sex and gore. Crowds flocked to the courtroom in their best theater clothes.

Polly was acquitted in her Staten Island trial, which took place at the county courthouse in Historic Richmond Town. A second trial took place in Manhattan several blocks from P. T. Barnum's American Museum on Broadway near Fulton Street. While Polly was on trial facing the death penalty, Barnum dubbed her "The Witch of Staten Island" and constructed a wax tableau of a wizened, toothless hag, hacking her victims to bits with an ax—though Polly was actually quite young. Convicted in Manhattan, Polly spent two years in jail facing the gallows before she was finally acquitted in a third trial. Upon learning of her freedom, she immediately turned to her lawyer and asked, "Can't I sue Barnum now?"

Bigfoot in Staten Island

On the night of January 21, 1975, a Mrs. D. Daly was driving home near Richmond Town when she screeched to a stop, narrowly missing a six-foot-tall "bigfoot" exiting the church parking lot and heading for a garbage dump. The dumpster sighting led one bigfoot researcher, Tom Modern, to dub the creature Trashquatch, as opposed to Sasquatch, the notorious cryptid that baffles cryptozoologists in the Pacific Northwest and elsewhere.

Mrs. Daly's near miss was the second bigfoot sighting that day and the third in two months. Earlier that morning, a couple spotted an unusually furry biped in a church parking lot. In their *Bigfoot Casebook*, Janet and Colin Bord also recount that two boys wandering in the woods on December 7, 1974, nearly ran into a creature they described as a tall upright bear that howled at them.

Perhaps the bear missed the ferry and had to swim from downtown Manhattan. Personally, I find it hard to believe in a mammal that has left no trace in the fossil record and has never turned up as road kill.

From Landfill to Landmark
Freshkills Park

What's the largest human-made structure on Earth?

From 1991 to 2001, it was Fresh Kills Landfill in Staten Island—a 2,200-acre (4.6 square-mile) mound of garbage, visible from space. Opened in 1948, Fresh Kills received twenty barges, each bearing 650 tons of NYC's municipal waste per day. The pile's peak reached about 385 feet—that's 80 feet higher than the Statue of Liberty—fit for a

⋆ ⋆

King Kong–size Oscar the Grouch. If it were still open today, Fresh Kills Landfill would be the tallest point on the East Coast. Fortunately, that distinction goes to the 410-foot Todt Hill, also on Staten Island.

On May 22, 2001, NYC closed the landfill—as Staten Island residents had been demanding for years. But this wasn't the end. On the night of September 12, 2001, Fresh Kills became a crime scene, as the city transported 1.8 million tons of crushed steel and debris from Ground Zero to the landfill's West Park. By 2002, thousands of forensic detectives had already clocked over 1.7 million hours to hand-sift the ruins for personal effects and human remains, including 4,257 human remains, leading to the identification of more than 300 individuals, roughly 4,000 personal photographs, $78,318.47 in currencies from around the world, 54,000 drivers licenses and other personal identification items, 1,358 vehicles including 102 from the fire department and 61 from the police department. In early 2010, Fresh Kills received another 844 cubic yards of material from a sub-basement of one of the twin towers.

The city plans to build a monument to September 11 at the site of this investigation. Meanwhile, the rest of the erstwhile landfill is being converted into a public recreational area called Freshkills Park. The portmanteau word *Freshkills* is deliberate. It seems the City needed to change the name to distinguish *Freshkills* Park from *Fresh Kills* landfill. They're keeping the name, since in Middle Dutch *kille* meant "riverbed" or "water channel." "Fresh Kills" never referred to road kill.

Freshkills Park lies on Staten Island's western shore along the Arthur Kill, the tidal strait that separates Staten Island from New Jersey. At 2,200 acres, it will be 2.5 times the size of Central Park. From April through November, you can take a free tour leaving from the Eltingville Transit Center at 90-98 Wainwright Avenue, near the intersection of Arthur Kill Road and Richmond Avenue. For construction updates and information on tours, talks, and other public programs, go to: www.nyc govparks.org/sub_your_park/fresh_kills_park/html/fresh_kills_park.html, or www.freshkillspark.wordpress.com.

★ ★

The Burger King Peacock

A peacock waddled into the parking lot of a Staten Island Burger King on June 28, 2007. As astounded burger flippers fed the bird hamburger buns, a bedraggled-looking man stormed into the parking lot, grabbed the peacock by the neck, and hurled it onto the asphalt.

"I'm killing a vampire," he screeched, as he beat the bird to death, then ran off.

The story made it into a small-town newspaper in Virginia, where former Staten Islander Charles Johnson read about the slain peacock and decided to rehabilitate New York's reputation.

A retired high school industrial arts teacher, Johnson carved a life-size statue of a peacock from a piece of elm and decorated it with real peacock feathers. The work now stands in a corner of the Burger King. The plaque reads: MEMORIAL TO BURGER KING PEACOCK. MADE AND DONATED BY PRHS [PORT RICHMOND HIGH SCHOOL] I.A. RETIRED TEACHER CHARLES JOHNSON.

The peacock memorial occupies an honorable place beside the counter of the Burger King at 7001 Amboy Road in the Tottenville Shopping Center, way out near the southwestern tip of Staten Isand. If you're going to make the trek, combine it with a trip to the nearby Conference House where Ben Franklin, John Adams, and Edward Rutledge met with the British, but refused to withdraw the Declaration of Independence. On the way to the Burger King, you can also stop by the rock marking the Rose and Crown Tavern at Richmond Road and New Dorp Lane, where British general William Howe supposedly read the Declaration of Independence to his officers in 1776.

To contact the Burger King, call (718) 948-9689.

Even with Charles Johnson's *Memorial to Burger King Peacock*, peacocks have avoided the fast-food joint—probably for fear of becoming a TenderCrisp Peacock Sandwich.

9

The New York City Subway

It's sometimes easy to forget what's right under our feet, but where would we New Yorkers be without the subway? Roughly five million people per weekday and 1.58 billion per year wait at the 468 stations and ride the 27 lines. Without the subway, we'd all be stuck in traffic—or working online, ordering FreshDirect, and hanging out with friends on Facebook and Skype.

New Yorkers often speak of the subway as the city's lifeblood or circulatory system—a vast, vital web of arteries and veins under the urban skin. The subway is also a great leveler. People of all classes and hundreds of ethnic and immigrant groups commingle. Since the subway is often quicker than a car or limo, celebrities and billionaires sometimes wait on the platform with the rest of us. And, aside from priority seating for the disabled, no one gets special treatment. The doors shut on the rich and renowned as surely as the poor and unknown. Samuel L. Jackson once got a foot stuck in the closing doors. (This was several years before his breakout role in Pulp Fiction, but fame wouldn't have opened doors for him in this case.)

The first subway line—from City Hall to 145th Street and Broadway—opened on October 27, 1904. In the 1920s and 1930s, NYC had three separate subway systems, including two private companies, the Interborough Rapid Transit Company (IRT) and Brooklyn-Manhattan Transit Corporation (BMT), and the city-owned Independent Subway System (IND). In 1940, the New York City Board of Transportation merged the

★ ★

IRT, BMT, and IND to form the New York City subway system. A long, complicated history joined subway, streetcars, buses, bridges, and tunnels under the watchful eye of the Metropolitan Transportation Authority (MTA) that we know and love today.

To learn more about the subway, visit the New York Transit Museum. As you board the vintage subway cars in the Moving the Millions exhibit, trail politely behind some native New Yorkers and listen to them reminisce: "I remember this car! My grandfather used to take me to the Yankees game . . ."

Located in downtown Brooklyn at the corner of Boerum Place and Schermerhorn Street, the New York Transit Museum is open Tuesday through Friday 10:00 a.m. to 4:00 p.m. and Saturday and Sunday noon to 5:00 p.m. For more info, go to www.mta.info/mta/museum, or call (718) 694-1600.

★ ★

Sand Hogs

The process of constructing subway tunnels has changed dramatically in the last century. Since the 1950s, moles, also known as tunnel-boring machines (TBMs), have burrowed through the ground like earthworms. But in the early 1900s, workers excavated tunnels by digging, or by drilling and blasting hard rock. Some laborers called sand hogs specialized in toiling under the most grueling and treacherous conditions. During underwater tunneling, workers risked floods, rockslides, dynamite accidents, lung diseases, decompression sickness (aka "the bends"), and "blowouts."

Under rivers tunnels were pressurized to keep water out. In a blowout, compressed air starts leaking out through a weak spot in the tunnel's roof. As the air rushes out, like air escaping from a balloon, workers can get sucked out of the tunnel.

On February 19, 1916, a blowout occurred in a tunnel under the East River near the end of Brooklyn's Montague Street. The force of the air blew one worker through twelve feet of dirt, then through the river itself, and finally propelled him into the air. Witnesses said that twenty-eight-year-old Marshall Mabey shot up twenty feet into the air on the top of a geyser. Mabey told reporters he'd heard about another sandhog, Dick Creedon, who had survived an under-river tunnel blowout in 1905. When Mabey realized he was about to get sucked out of the tunnel, he took a quick breath and shut his mouth tight. According to some reports, he described the force of the suction that pulled him through the riverbed: "I was being held tight . . . tighter than any girl ever held me."

Creedon's blowout happened in the Joralemon Street Tunnel, which now carries the 4 and 5 trains beneath the East River between Manhattan and Brooklyn; Mabey's took place in the Montague Tunnel, through which the M, R, and N trains travel under the East River. When you take these trains, remember Creedon and Mabey.

"The Mona Lisa of Subway Stations"
City Hall Station

When we think of a subway, most of us picture a dusty underground tunnel, not a masterpiece hanging in a museum. But City Hall station under City Hall Park was dubbed the Mona Lisa of Subway Stations. The New York–based architectural firm Heins and LaFarge designed the station in Romanesque Revival style with skylights, chandeliers, and Spanish architect Rafael Guastavino's signature vaults, built with terra-cotta tiles interlocked in a herringbone pattern.

For recent photos, check out Kevin Walsh's fascinating chronicle of his visit at www.forgotten-ny.com/SUBWAYS/newcityhall/newcityhall.html. City Hall Station features Rafael Guastavino's Tile Arch System, also used to build Grand Central's Whispering Gallery below.
DETROIT PUBLISHING COMPANY, LIBRARY OF CONGRESS

★ ★

Opening on October 27, 1904, City Hall Station was the terminus of the first IRT subway line and its crowning jewel. Unfortunately, the tiny station with its sharply curved platform couldn't accommodate the longer subway cars that joined the fleet in the 1940s. There was too much space between the center doors on the subway cars and the platform edge.

The station was closed in 1945. Since then, it has only been used as a loop for the 6 train to turn around after its last downtown stop at Brooklyn Bridge. You can see the skylights in City Hall Park.

If you'd like to visit the station in a leisurely manner, become a member of the New York Transit Museum, which offers members-only tours several times a year. Alternatively, you can take the split-second free tour by staying on the downtown 6 train past its last stop at Brooklyn Bridge. Simply ignore the automated voice that says, "This is the last stop on this train. Everybody please exit the train." If you keep your eyes peeled, you'll get a quick glimpse of City Hall Station. But it's not a great photo opportunity. The station is dark and the train zooms past, so you'll miss it if you blink.

Oculus by Kristen Jones and Andrew Ginzel
Park Place/Chambers Street—World Trade Center Subway Stations

All eyes are on you, and I'm not just talking about surveillance cameras and security guards. At rush hour, in busy stations like this one, you'll pass hundreds, sometimes thousands of eyes per day. Strangers avert their gaze, but if you're not reading a book or newspaper, the subway car can be a viewing gallery.

Artists Kristen Jones and Andrew Ginzel photographed the eyes of twelve hundred New Yorkers and created *Oculus*. Distributed through three interconnected stations, three hundred stone mosaic eyes—each roughly a foot in width—peer out from the white tile walls, as if windows had been cut in the station, and giants were peeking in from outside. Near the entrance on Park Place between Church Street and Broadway lies a 40-by-20-foot elliptical glass and stone floor mosaic:

Stone mosaic eyes gaze out from the walls and floor of the Park Place/Chambers Street–World Trade Center Station.

OCULUS, 1998, © KRISTEN JONES AND ANDREW GINZEL. COMMISSIONED AND OWNED BY MTA ARTS FOR TRANSIT. PHOTO BY LISA MONTANARELLI.

A single disembodied eye gazes up from the center of an vortex with maps of NYC and the continents against an ultramarine background. The eyes of the subway station never blink, because the subway never sleeps.

On their website (www.jonesginzel.com), Kristin Jones and Andrew Ginzel mention that the *Wall Street Journal* recognized *Oculus* as "an unexpected monument," after the mosaics survived the September 11 attacks, which damaged the World Trade Center Station.

Light Bulb Theft Prevention on the New York Subway

Before 1940 (and the widespread use of fluorescent lighting), New York subway cars had incandescent light bulbs. These bulbs were within easy reach on the car's low ceiling, so passengers were tempted to steal them to use in their lamps at home. To prevent petty theft, bulbs for subway cars were designed differently from regular incandescent light bulbs: They screwed in counterclockwise instead of clockwise and ran on DC rather than current. In other words, if a passenger took a bulb home from the subway, he wouldn't be able to screw it into the socket, and even if he did, it wouldn't work.

Trivia

In New York State, a couple "cannot dissolve a marriage for irreconcilable differences, unless they both agree to it."

The Steinway Tunnel and U Thant Island

Under the East River and in the East River just south of Roosevelt Island

You might think an island couldn't be part of the subway. While this may be true, subway construction debris can an island make. In the 1890s, piano manufacturer William Steinway was building a tunnel under the East River from his company in Queens to Manhattan. (The product of these labors, the Steinway Tunnel, now carries the 7 trains between Manhattan's Grand Central/Forty-Second Street subway station and the Vernon Boulevard-Jackson Avenue stop in Queens.)

During construction, workers dug a shaft to the tunnels down an existing outcrop called Man-o'-War Reef and used landfill from the shaft to make the reef into a 100-by-200-foot islet. The islet was officially named Belmont Island after financier August Belmont Jr., who finished the tunnels after Steinway died.

The few people who know of the island call it U Thant, rather than Belmont. In 1977, a group called *Sri Chinmoy: The Peace Meditation at the United Nations* leased NYC's tiniest islet from New York State, planted greenery, and dedicated the island to Burmese diplomat Pantanaw U Thant, who served as the third U.N. secretary general from 1961 to 1971. The group also installed a "oneness arch" with a time-capsule containing U Thant's personal items and speeches.

I don't recommend visiting the island, because it's illegal. But you can see it from the southern tip of Roosevelt Island, from the United

Nations and nearby sections of the FDR Drive, and from Gantry Plaza State Park in Queens.

During the 2004 Republican National Convention, Brooklyn artist Duke Riley rowed out to U Thant Island under cover of night, planted a flag, and declared it a sovereign nation. This gesture has never caught on, partly because the island's only residents are double-crested cormorants, who don't care much about laws or national boundaries.

Life Underground by Tom Otterness
Fourteenth Street/Eighth Avenue Subway Station

An alligator clad in a business suit and bow tie pokes his snout out of a manhole and clamps his teeth around a man with a moneybag for a head. This hallucinatory scene is part of Tom Otterness's public artwork *Life Underground* (2001)—over one hundred cast-bronze sculptures installed in the Fourteenth Street/Eighth Avenue subway station.

The manhole scene riffs on the classic NYC urban legend propagated by Thomas Pynchon's 1963 novel, *V.* Hapless tourists brought cute baby alligators home from Florida and flushed them down the toilet when it was no longer fun to take a bath with a baby alligator. The crocodilians survived and bred in NYC sewers, where they wait to gobble unsuspecting pedestrians.

In *Life Underground*, the alligator has human hands and sports a business suit, while the moneybag-headed man caught in the gator's jaws recalls the nineteenth-century political cartoons of Boss Tweed—doyen of the Tammany Hall political machine that pulled the purse strings of New York when the city's first subway was forged. Otterness seems to say that the real "alligator in the sewer" is the boss-eat-boss world of corporate elites devouring each other.

Although Otterness criticizes capitalism, he also knows that—as a prolific public artist crafting high-priced commodities bought and sold on the art market—he isn't outside the system he critiques. Cast-bronze sculptures aren't cheap to produce: The Arts for Transit

Will the real alligator in the sewer please stand up?
LIFE UNDERGROUND, 2001, © TOM OTTERNESS. COMMISSIONED AND OWNED BY MTA ARTS FOR TRANSIT. PHOTO BY LISA MONTANARELLI.

program of the Metropolitan Transportation Authority (MTA) commissioned *Life Underground* for $200,000, and that's only one of Otterness's many installations throughout the United States and Europe. The process of having one's art approved and installed in public venues requires a knack for navigating the proper channels and prostrating oneself before government agencies, real estate developers, and other deep-pocketed authorities.

Otterness is quite canny about the conditions under which he practices his craft. In one piece from *Life Underground*, a woman reading a book sits on the round belly of a rich financier, lying spread-eagle on a

★ ★

pile of coins. The point is that cultural pursuits require capital. It's hard to make cast-bronze sculptures if you labor 24-7 just to pay the rent.

To experience *Life Underground*, enter the Fourteenth Street/Eighth Avenue subway station at the corner of Eighth Avenue and Fourteenth, Fifteenth, or Sixteenth Street.

Moving Under the Hudson River
North River Tunnels

If you've taken Amtrak or New Jersey Transit from Weehawken, New Jersey to Manhattan's Pennsylvania Station, you've traveled through the North River tunnels. Buried deep beneath the Hudson River, these 6,000-foot-long, cast-iron tubes carry hundreds of thousands of commuters each day.

Did you know that these tunnels *move*?

In 1907, while the tunnels were still under construction, the engineers made the horrifying discovery that the tubes were shifting downward. What if they kept sinking into the silt until they cracked open?

One Million Pounds of Train

A subway car weighs between 75,000 and 90,000 pounds. The heaviest parts are the motor trucks, which weigh 25,000 pounds each. Each motor truck includes an electric motor, a braking system, wheels—everything involved in making the car move. A ten-car train with passengers can weigh nearly one million pounds.

Trivia

It is legal for both men and women to ride the New York City subway naked from the waist up.

Conducting careful studies, the engineers determined that the Hudson's powerful tides were affecting the tubes: Though they were deep under the riverbed, the tunnels rose when the tide fell and fell when it rose.

The engineers debated whether to install supports to hold the tubes in place. In the end, they decided to do nothing and let the tunnels move with the tides. The North River tunnels opened in 1910, and the tunnels have safely relayed commuters between Manhattan and New Jersey ever since.

Whispering Gallery
Grand Central Oyster Bar and Restaurant at Grand Central Terminal, Forty-Second Street and Park Avenue

Where can you go for a quiet conversation in Grand Central during rush hour? Take a friend to the tiled vaults in front of the Oyster Bar, stand at diagonally opposite corners, and whisper into the tiles. If your friend puts his ear to the pillar, he'll hear your words as distinctly as if you stood face to face, but no one else will hear you. The trick works because curved surfaces can reflect and focus sound in much the same way that curved mirrors focus light. But you have to whisper. If you speak at your regular volume, your words will reverberate—bouncing back and forth repeatedly, so your listener won't be able to distinguish them.

When Grand Central was built in 1913, Spanish architect Rafael Guastavino and his son, Rafael Guastavino Jr., of the Guastavino

★ ★

Fireproof Construction Company designed the whispering gallery based on architectural principles that have been used for centuries worldwide—from the dome of St. Paul's Cathedral in London to the Temple of Heaven in Beijing to the Gol Gumbaz in Bijapur, India.

According to the Oyster Bar's staff, scores of marriage proposals echo across the vaults each day. (The staff knows because some newly engaged couples stop in the bar for post-proposal drinks and share their good news.)

The next time you're in Grand Central with a friend, try out the Whispering Gallery. Just make sure your confidante has her ear to the

**Grand Central Terminal's Whispering Gallery.
Photo intentionally blurred to protect the guilty.**

pillar diagonally opposite from you. There are no posted instructions, so if you're unsure what to do, simply wait in the vault for a few minutes. Soon enough, a pair of people will head to opposite corners and whisper into the tiles.

A word of caution: If you're dining in the Oyster Bar, don't try to have a confidential conversation near an archway. The Oyster Bar has the same vaulted ceilings, and your secrets may carry across the room.

Globetrotting on the Number 7 Subway Line
The IRT 7 Train, also known as The International Express

It's not every day that a subway line earns the distinction of national landmark, but in 2000 the White House designated the IRT 7 line as one of sixteen National Millennium Trails representing the American immigrant experience. The route—from Flushing in Queens to Times Square in Manhattan—passes Afghan, Armenian, Bangladeshi, Chinese, Colombian, Indian, Irish, Italian, Korean, Mexican, Pakistani, Romanian, Spanish, Thai, Turkish, and Uruguayan enclaves, just to name a sampling.

This is no coincidence: In the early 1900s, a huge number of immigrants still lived in overcrowded Lower East Side tenements. The City built the 7 line partly to allow these immigrants to move to Queens, so they could have a better quality of life as well as a fast, inexpensive commute to work. Many immigrant groups settled along the route of the 7 train. Even today, roughly half of Queens residents are foreign-born, and a large percentage of these immigrants choose to live in the borough's northwest part, serviced by the 7.

Although you can't exactly travel around the world on the 7 train, you can sit or stand next to people from many lands and politely glance over their shoulders at their foreign-language newspapers. But even more important, you can take the 7 to explore a wide variety of ethnic and immigrant neighborhoods. Check out the introduction to the Queens chapter for some ideas.

In Manhattan, the 7 makes three stops along Forty-Second Street: Times Square, Fifth Avenue/Bryant Park, and Grand Central. You're

★ ★

The Department of City Planning calls the 7
the International Express because it travels through
so many immigrant and ethnic enclaves.

underground in Manhattan, but in Queens the 7 runs on elevated tracks—often with spectacular urban views. Between the stations at Hunters Point Avenue and Forty-Fifth Road/Courthouse Square in Long Island City, look for 5Pointz Aerosol Art Center (www.5ptz .com), a 200,000-square-foot factory building that graffiti artists from around the world have covered with murals. The 7 train also stops in Woodside, in Jackson Heights, at Flushing Meadows Corona Park, and at the Mets' Citi Field stadium on its way to Main Street/Flushing. Woodside and Jackson Heights both have predominantly foreign-born residents. Woodside has a Little Manila, as well as large Chinese, Columbian, Dominican, Korean, Irish, Mexican, and Muslim populations. Jackson Heights is home to a Little India and communities of immigrants from Argentina, Colombia, and Uruguay.

The Life and Afterlife of an NYC Subway Car

Subway cars have an average lifespan of thirty-five to forty-five years, but some of the older cars remained in use much longer. In 1903, the Brooklyn Rapid Transit Company (BRT) ordered one hundred motorized cars for the Brooklyn Union Elevated Railroad. Some die-hard members of this group traveled the tracks from 1904 to 1969. At the New York Transit Museum at Boerum Place and Schermerhorn Street in Brooklyn, you can climb inside the oldest operational member of the museum's fleet: Car 1273, built in 1904.

Nowadays, worn-out subway cars are sent out to sea. Literally. De-greased and stripped of their doors, windows, and wheels, the eighteen-ton, stainless steel cars are stacked on a barge and dumped into the waters along the coasts of New Jersey, Delaware, and Maryland. The mid-Atlantic coastal seabed is mostly bare sand—offering little protection for fish. The subway cars serve as artificial reefs, where fish can hide from their predators, lay eggs safely, and feed on the crabs, shrimp, and mussels that flock to the reefs.

At the New York Transit Museum, step inside the oldest operational subway car, built in 1904.

bibliography

Anbinder, Tyler. *Five Points*. New York: Penguin Group, 2001.

Anderson, Brooke Davis, Director and Curator of the Contemporary Center at the American Folk Art Museum. "Audiotour: *In the Realms of the Unreal*." www.pbs.org/pov/intherealms/audiotour.php (accessed January 3, 2010).

Apollo Theater. "Amateur Night," www.apollotheater.org/amateur night.htm#about (accessed June 19, 2010).

Beloff, Zoe. Zoe Beloff website. www.zoebeloff.com (accessed April 11, 2010).

Bianco, Anthony. *Ghosts of 42nd Street: A History of America's Most Infamous Block*. New York: William Morrow, 2004.

The Bowery Boys (Greg Young and Tom Meyers). "Coney Island Part 1: Playground of the World." The Bowery Boys Podcast. http://itunes .apple.com/podcast/nyc-history-bowery-boys-archive/id293257920 (accessed February 10, 2010).

———. "Coney Island Part 1: Playground of the World." The Bowery Boys Podcast. http://itunes.apple.com/podcast/nyc-history-bowery -boys-archive/id293257920 (accessed February 10, 2010).

———. "Coney Island Part 2: 20th Century Sideshow." The Bowery Boys Podcast. http://itunes.apple.com/podcast/nyc-history-bowery -boys-archive/id293257920 (accessed February 10, 2010).

———. "Five Points, Part 1." The Bowery Boys Podcast. http://the boweryboys.blogspot.com/2008/08/podcast-five-points-wicked-slum .html (accessed February 8, 2010).

———. "Five Points, Part 2." The Bowery Boys Podcast. http://the boweryboys.blogspot.com/2008/08/podcast-fate-of-five-points.html (accessed February 8, 2010).

———. "Grant's Tomb." The Bowery Boys Podcast. http://thebowery boys.blogspot.com/2008/05/podcast-grant-tomb.html (accessed March 16, 2010).

———. "The Guggenheim Museum." The Bowery Boys Podcast. http://theboweryboys.blogspot.com/2008/10/podcast-guggenheim -museum.html (accessed March 4, 2010).

bibliography

———. "Henry Ward Beecher and Plymouth Church." The Bowery Boys Podcast. http://theboweryboys.blogspot.com/2008/03/henry-ward-beecher-and-plymouth-church.html (accessed March 23, 2010).

———. "The New York Stock Exchange." The Bowery Boys Podcast. http://theboweryboys.blogspot.com/2008/09/podcast-new-york-stock-exchange.html (accessed April 5, 2010).

———. "P.T. Barnum's American Museum." The Bowery Boys Podcast. http://theboweryboys.blogspot.com/2008/05/podcast-barnum-american-museum.html (accessed March 18, 2010).

———. "Pennsylvania Station: Manhattan's Missing Treasure." The Bowery Boys Podcast. http://theboweryboys.blogspot.com/2009/04/pennsylvania-station-podcast.html (accessed March 23, 2010).

———. "Staten Island: A Brief History." The Bowery Boys Podcast, http://theboweryboys.blogspot.com/2007/11/staten-island-brief-history.html (accessed February 5, 2010).

———. "Ziegfeld!" The Bowery Boys Podcast. http://theboweryboys.blogspot.com/2009/01/podcast-ziegfeld.html (accessed March 18, 2010).

Brick, Michael. "And Next to the Bearded Lady, Premature Babies." New York Times, June 12, 2005, N.Y./ Region section, www.nytimes.com/2005/06/12/nyregion/12coney.html (accessed April 10, 2010).

Burrows, Edwin G. and Mike Wallace. Gotham: A History of New York to 1898. London: Oxford University Press, 2000.

Bush, Melanie, "Miss Subways, Subversive and Sublime," New York Times, October 24, 2004, N.Y./ Region section, www.nytimes.com/2004/10/24/nyregion/thecity/24subw.html (accessed May 7, 2010).

Carducci, Vince. "Tom Otterness: Public Art and the Civic Ideal in the Postmodern Age." Sculpture 24, no. 3 (April 2005) www.sculpture.org/documents/scmag05/april_05/otterness/otterness.shtml (accessed November 27, 2009).

The Cathedral of St. John the Divine. www.stjohndivine.org (accessed May 16, 2010).

Chan, Sewell. "A Translucent Wire in the Sky." June 15, 2007, http://cityroom.blogs.nytimes.com/2007/06/15/a-translucent-wire-in-the-sky/(accessed April 25, 2010).

bibliography

Chen, Wellington. Executive Director Chinatown Partnership LDC, "New York Beyond Site: Columbus Park Pavilion," www.nybeyondsight.org/columbus-park-pavilion.shtml (accessed May 5, 2010).

Cohen, Bille. "Next Stop: No. 7 Train From Flushing-Main Street to Times Square." *New York Times,* January 14, 2008, Real Estate section, www.nytimes.com/2008/01/14/realestate/14comm.html (accessed May 9, 2010).

Cohen, Gabriel. "For You, Half Price," *New York Times*, November 27, 2005, N.Y./ Region section, www.nytimes.com/2005/11/27/nyregion/thecity/27brid.html (accessed May 9, 2010).

Cook, Nick. *Roller Coasters: Or I Had So Much Fun, I Almost Puked.* Minneapolis, MN: Carolrhoda Books, 1998.

"Duke Riley: Those About to Die Salute You." Queens Museum of Art. www.queensmuseum.org/duke-riley-those-about-to-die-salute-you (accessed April 2, 2010).

"Dumb State Laws," www.usattorneylegalservices.com/dumb-state-laws.html (accessed July 17, 2010).

Dunlap, David W. *On Broadway: A Journey Uptown Over Time*. New York: Rizzoli, 1990.

———. "Xanadus Rise to a Higher Calling," *New York Times*, April 13, 2001, Movies section, www.nytimes.com/2001/04/13/movies/xanadus-rise-to-a-higher-calling.html (accessed April 23, 2010).

Ellis, Edward Robb. *The Epic of New York City*. Old Town Books. New York: Basic Books, 2004.

"1520 Sedgwick Ave." www.placematters.net/node/959 (accessed May 10, 2010).

"1520 Sedgwick Ave. Honored by NYC Art Society as Hip-Hop Birthplace," www.theboombox.com/2009/12/02/1520-sedgwick-ave-honored-by-nyc-art-society-as-hip-hop-birthpl/ (accessed May 10, 2010).

Freedman, Samuel G. "On Religion: A Jewish Ritual Collides with Mother Nature," *New York Times*, March 5, 2010, U.S. section, www.nytimes.com/2010/03/06/us/06religion.html (accessed April 21, 2010).

bibliography

"Fresh Kills Landfill," http://acc6.its.brooklyn.cuny.edu/~scintech/solid /silandfill.html (accessed November 29, 2009).

Gethard, Chris. *Weird New York: Your Travel Guide to New York's Local Legends and Best Kept Secrets*. Mark Moran and Mark Sceurman, Executive Editors. New York: Sterling Publishing Co., 2005.

Goetz, Robert F. "If You're Thinking of Living In: Marble Hill." *New York Times*, February 19, 1989, Real Estate section, www.nytimes .com/1989/02/19/realestate/if-you-re-thinking-of-living-in-marble-hill .html (accessed April 15, 2010).

Gordon, Jerry, DDS. "George Washington's False Teeth." www .dentistry.com/treatments/dentures/george-washingtons-false-teeth (accessed May 6, 2010).

Hawley, Joshua David. *Theodore Roosevelt: Preacher of Righteousness*. New Haven: Yale University Press, 2008.

Hayes, Holly. "Cathedral of St. John the Divine, New York City." Sacred Destinations. www.sacred-destinations.com/usa/new-york-city -cathedral-st-john-the-divine (accessed May 16, 2010).

"Henry Ward Beecher." Plymouth Church of the Pilgrims. www.plymouth church.org/our_history_henry-wardbeecher.php (accessed March 17, 2010).

"History of New York Geology," www.newyorknature.net/Geology.html (accessed June 22, 2010).

Humor Sites. www.bored.com/humor (accessed July 13, 2010).

Hurdle, Jon. "New York Subway Cars Find New Life on the Ocean Floor." Reuters. www.reuters.com/article/idUSN1643767620080517 (accessed January 31, 2010).

"The International Express: Around the World On the 7 Train." *Queens Tribune*, Anniversary 2002. www.queenstribune.com/anniversary 2002/ internationalexpress.htm (accessed May 12, 2010).

"Islamic Cultural Center (Mosque)." www.nyc-architecture.com/UES/ UES091.htm (accessed May 2, 2010).

bibliography

Johnson, Caitlin A. "The Evolution Of Peking Duck: Peking Duck Was Once Only Consumed by Emperors, Now It's Available to All." www.cbsnews.com/stories/2006/09/24/sunday/main2036347.shtml (accessed January 30, 2010).

Johnson, John H. *Fact Not Fiction in Harlem.* St. Martin's Church, 1980.

Jones, Kristin and Andrew Ginzel. "Oculus: Description." Kristin Jones–Andrew Ginzel website, www.jonesginzel.com (accessed May 8, 2010).

Jonnes, Jill. *Conquering Gotham: A Gilded Age Epic: The Construction of Penn Station and its Tunnels.* New York: Viking, 2007.

"King Jagiello." The Official Website of Central Park. www.central parknyc.org/visit/things-to-see/great-lawn/king-jagiello.html (accessed May 17, 2010).

Knutson, Lawrence L. "Alice Roosevelt Longworth, wild thing." *Salon.* www.salon.com/people/feature/1999/06/07/longworth/index .html (accessed December 17, 2009).

"La Guardia Pays Tribute to Poland." *New York Times*, October 12, 1939, http://select.nytimes.com/mem/archive/pdf?res=F40B1EFA3F5A 177A93C0A8178BD95F4D8385F9 (accessed May 17, 2010).

Marx, Rebecca. "Achieve Closure." *New York* magazine. http://nymag .com/nymetro/bony/n_9907 (accessed May 17, 2010).

Mindlin, Alex. "String Theory," *New York Times*, March 26, 2006, N.Y./ Region section, www.nytimes.com/2006/03/26/nyregion /thecity/26eruv.html (accessed April 10, 2010).

Moss, Jeremiah. "Coney Psychoanalytic." Jeremiah's Vanishing New York. http://vanishingnewyork.blogspot.com/2009/08/coney-psycho analytic.html (accessed April 10, 2010).

———. "Zoe Beloff." Jeremiah's Vanishing New York. http://vanishing newyork.blogspot.com/2009/08/zoe-beloff.html (accessed April 17, 2010).

Nash, Jay Robert. *Hustlers and Con Men: An Anecdotal History of the Confidence Man and His Games.* M. Evans & Co., 1976.

bibliography

New York City Department of City Planning. "Current Population Esti-mates." The Official Website of New York City. www.nyc.gov /html/dcp/html/census/popcur.shtml (accessed March 7, 2010).

"New York's Urban Jungle." www.nydailynews.com/news /galleries/new_yorks_urban_jungle/new_yorks_urban_jungle .html#ixzz0nbpJcScx (accessed May 14, 2010).

Nikki D., "A visitor's guide to New York City's oddball laws," www .helium.com/items/628475-a-visitors-guide-to-new-york-citys-oddball-laws (accessed July 21, 2010).

Pollack, Michael. "F.Y.I." *New York Times*. August 1, 2004, N.Y./ Region section, www.nytimes.com/2004/08/01/nyregion/fyi-480444 .html (accessed May 1, 2010).

Ramirez, Anthony. "After a 28-Year Hiatus, Miss (er, Ms.) Subways Is Back." *New York Times*, October 26, 2004, N.Y./ Region section, www.nytimes.com/2004/10/26/nyregion/26subway.html (accessed May 13, 2010).

Rasenberger, Jim. "City Lore: The Witch of Staten Island." *New York Times*, October 29, 2000, N.Y./Region section, www.nytimes .com/2000/10/29/nyregion/city-lore-the-witch-of-staten-island.html (accessed March 24, 2010).

Reaven, Marci and Steve Zeitlin. *Hidden New York: A Guide to Places that Matter*. New Brunswick, NJ: Rutgers University Press, 2006.

Reisman, Suzanne. *Off the Beaten (Subway) Track: New York City's Best Unusual Attractions*. Nashville, TN: Cumberland House, 2008.

Renner, James. "Spuyten Duyvil Creek and the Harlem River Ship Canal," August 2005, www.washington-heights.us/history/archives/ spuyten_duyvil_creek_and_the_harlem_river_ship_canal_125.html (accessed April 21, 2010).

Riis, Jacob. *How the Other Half Lives*. www.authentichistory.com/1865-1897/progressive/riis/index.html (accessed February 23, 2010).

Riley, Duke. Duke Riley website. www.dukeriley.info (accessed April 2, 2010).

bibliography

★ ★

Roberts, Sam. "Listening to (and Saving) the World's Languages," *New York Times*, April 29, 2010, N.Y./ Region section, www.nytimes .com/2010/04/29/nyregion/29lost.html (accessed on May 17, 2010).

Rogers, Thomas. "Competitive Eating: The Most American Sport?" *Salon*. www.salon.com/food/feature/2010/03/25/competitive _eating_ryan_nerz (accessed April 10, 2010).

Rose-Redwood, Reuben Skye. "Rationalizing the Landscape: Superimposing the Grid upon the Island of Manhattan." MS thesis, Pennsylvania State University, 2002.

Sagalyn, Lynne B. *Times Square Roulette: Remaking the City Icon*. Cambridge: MIT Press, 2001.

Saint George's Church website. www.sg1702.org/english/about.htm

Saltz, Jerry. "Duke Riley's Insane Triumph." *Artnet Magazine*. www.artnet.com/magazineus/features/saltz/duke-riley8-17-09.asp (accessed April 2, 2010).

"Samuel L. Jackson awarded $540,000 after being dragged by New York subway train in 1988." *Jet,* May 27, 1996. http://findarticles.com/p /articles/mi_m1355/is_n2_v90/ai_18342971/ (accessed May 17, 2010).

Santé, Luc. *Low Life: Lures and Snares of Old New York*. New York: Farrar, Straus and Giroux, 2003.

Schneider, Daniel B. "F.Y.I. Bronx River Sentry." *New York Times*, September 3, 2000, N.Y./ Region section, www.nytimes.com/2000 /09/03/ nyregion/fyi-928437.html (accessed April 9, 2010).

Sifakis, Carl. "Hoaxes and Scams: A Compendium of Deceptions, Ruses and Swindles." New York: Facts on File, 1994.

Stanton, Jeffrey. "Coney Island: Disasters, Spectacles and Cycloramas." Coney Island History Site. www.westland.net/coneyisland/articles /shows.htm (accessed April 10, 2010).

Staten Island Museum. www.statenislandmuseum.org/articles/cPath-49/ About+Us.html (accessed March 28, 2010).

Strausbaugh, John. "The Case of Sigmund F. and Coney I.," *New York Times*, July 26, 2009, Arts section, www.nytimes.com/2009 /07/26/ arts/design/26strau.html (accessed April 10, 2010).

"Struggling Museum Now Allowing Patrons to Touch Paintings." *The Onion*, October 5, 2009, Issue 45:41, www.theonion.com/articles /struggling-museum-now-allowing-patrons-to-touch-pa,2821 (accessed December 29, 2009).

"Subway and Bus Ridership: Statistics 2009," Metropolitan Transportation Authority (MTA), http://mta.info/nyct/facts/ridership/index.htm (accessed on May 4, 2010).

"Tiger Owner Says He Sought Animal Haven," www.cnn.com/2003 /US /Northeast/10/13/harlem.tiger/ (accessed May 14, 2010).

"A Tiger's Keeper Says He Misses His 'Friend,'" *New York Times,* October 8, 2003, N.Y./Region section, www.nytimes.com/2003/10/08/ nyregion/08TIGE.html (accessed May 14, 2010).

Traub, James. *The Devil's Playground: A Century of Pleasure and Profit in Times Square*. New York: Random House, 2004.

Tyson, Neil deGrasse. "Manhattanhenge." Hayden Planetarium website. www.haydenplanetarium.org/resources/starstruck/manhattanhenge (accessed July 10, 2010).

U.S. Bureau of the Census. "Table 1. Rank by Population of the 100 Largest Urban Places, Listed Alphabetically by State: 1790–1990." June 15, 1998, www.census.gov/population/www/documentation /twps0027/tab01.txt (accessed May 13, 2010).

Wall, Diana diZerega and Anne-Marie Cantwell, *Touring Gotham's Archaeological Past: 8 Self-Guided Walking Tours through New York City*. New Haven and London: Yale, 2004.

Walsh, Kevin. *Forgotten New York*. New York: Collins Reference, 2006.

Waxman, Sharon. *Loot: The Battle Over the Stolen Treasures of the Ancient World.* New York: St. Martin's Press, 2008.

Wellborn, Mark. "Schumer to Lead Rally to Keep Birthplace of Hip Hop Affordable." *New York Observer*, July 23, 2007, www.observer .com/2007/birthplace-hip-hop-danger-losing-affordable -housing-label (accessed May 13, 2010).

index

index

index

index

★ ★

index

about the author

★ ★

Lisa Montanarelli has co-authored three nonfiction books, including *Strange But True San Francisco* and *Strange But True Chicago* (both Globe Pequot Press). She has contributed features, profiles, and reviews to *San Francisco Chronicle, Art and Antiques Magazine, California Literary Review*, *Colorado Review*, *Agence France-Presse,* and *Publishers Weekly*. She received her BA from Yale and her PhD in Comparative Literature from UC Berkeley. Visit her at www.LisaMontanarelli.com or www.LisaNY.com.